M.
2-6-87

EXPLORING
—THE—
COUNTRYSIDE

Editors: Vanessa Clarke
Kate Hayden · Barbara Taylor

Designer: Ben White

Illustrators: Wendy Bramall, Martin Camm,
Jeane Colville, Alan Male, Denys Ovenden,
Gordon Riley, Bernard Robinson, Norman
Weaver, Ann Winterbotham, David Wright

Picture Research: Jackie Cookson

Published in 1987 by Kingfisher Books Limited,
Elsley Court, 20–22 Great Titchfield Street,
London W1P 7AD
A Grisewood and Dempsey Company

The material in this book has previously been
published by Kingfisher Books Limited (1985) in four
separate volumes: Exploring the Countryside;
WOODLANDS, FIELDS AND HEDGEROWS,
SEASHORE, PONDS AND STREAMS,
PARKS AND GARDENS.

BRITISH LIBRARY CATALOGUING IN
PUBLICATION DATA
Chinery, Michael
Exploring the countryside.
1. Country life – Great Britain –
Juvenile literature
I. Title
941′.009′734
S522.G7

ISBN 0-86272-171-7

Phototypeset by Southern Positives and Negatives
(SPAN), Lingfield, Surrey
Colour separations by Newsele Litho, Milan
Printed in Italy by Vallardi Industrie Grafiche, Milan

EXPLORING
—THE—
COUNTRYSIDE

MICHAEL CHINERY

KINGFISHER BOOKS

Contents

The Living Landscape

Take a good look at the landscape around you the next time you are in the countryside. It is the stage on which all wildlife performs, and is therefore of considerable interest to the naturalist. Only by taking note of the surrounding landscape will you really understand why plants and animals live where they do. This is the basis of natural history or, to use its modern name, *ecology*.

Changing Scenery

Just like a theatre stage, the landscape has different kinds of scenery. Even on a short journey in the British Isles or other parts of Europe you will see several different types of scenery. Hills, valleys and plains form an ever-changing pattern as you travel along. Rivers, lakes, and seashores also contribute to the rich pattern of the countryside, as can you see in the picture below.

Many factors affect the shape of the landscape. The most important one is the nature of the underlying rocks. The hills and valleys that form the scenery are literally carved from the rocks by a variety of processes. Hard rocks tend to form rugged uplands, while softer rocks, such as chalk, form more 'comfortable' scenery, including the smoothly rounded hills of chalk downland.

Scenery not only changes from place to place; it also changes with time. Although you might think that hills and valleys are permanent features, they do not survive for ever. Landscapes are always changing through the continuous destruction of the rocks. The process is slow, but it is relentless. Rain beating on the rocks year after year dissolves some of the minerals and loosens the surface material, which is gradually swept into the rivers and carried away to the sea. Sand grains

Right: This village in the Netherlands is not a natural habitat for wildlife since the area has been greatly modified by people but there are still plenty of plants and animals living in the trees and gardens. Even the houses may contain a variety of insects and other small animals. There are many possibilities for nature study in such an area.

Rocks and Fossils

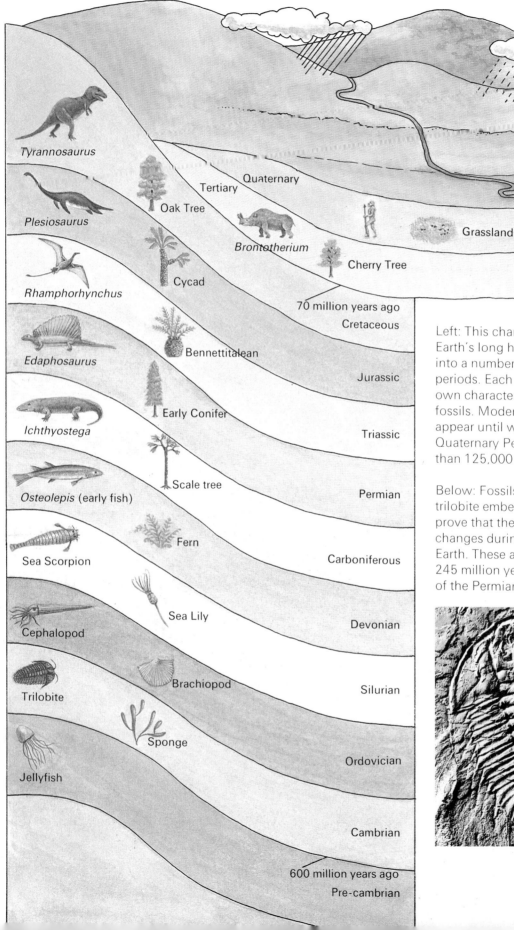

Tyrannosaurus

Plesiosaurus

Rhamphorhynchus

Edaphosaurus

Ichthyostega

Osteolepis (early fish)

Sea Scorpion

Cephalopod

Trilobite

Jellyfish

Oak Tree

Cycad

Bennettitalean

Early Conifer

Scale tree

Fern

Sea Lily

Brachiopod

Sponge

Quaternary

Tertiary

Brontotherium

Grassland

Cherry Tree

70 million years ago

Cretaceous

Jurassic

Triassic

Permian

Carboniferous

Devonian

Silurian

Ordovician

Cambrian

600 million years ago

Pre-cambrian

Left: This chart shows how the Earth's long history is divided into a number of geological time periods. Each time period has its own characteristic rocks and fossils. Modern humans did not appear until well into the Quaternary Period, little more than 125,000 years ago.

Below: Fossils such as this trilobite embedded in the rocks prove that there have been great changes during the history of the Earth. These animals died out 245 million years ago at the end of the Permian Period.

Mountains, Glaciers and Volcanoes

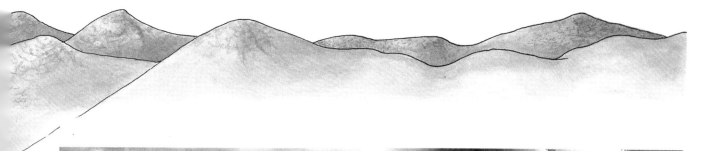

Above: Glaciers, such as this one in Iceland, are the remains of the huge sheets of ice that covered much of Europe in the Ice Age. If the climate became much colder, the ice could spread out again.

Above: Volcanoes can change the face of the land in a very short time. The ash and lava from this 1973 eruption on the Icelandic island of Heimaey swallowed up much of a town overnight.

and other materials are deposited there and eventually form a new generation of rocks. Rivers are particularly important in shaping the land. They don't just carry away loose material; they also carve valleys out of the rocks at the same time.

The erosion of the land is generally very slow and you won't normally see much change in your lifetime. But you can see the occasional sudden change; heavy rain or the sudden melting of snow can cause landslides in mountain areas and coastal cliffs sometimes collapse dramatically where they have been undercut by the waves.

The Ice Age
Ice is another important agent in shaping the land. Only 20,000 years ago – a short period compared with the age of the Earth – the climate was very much colder than it is now and much of Europe was covered with ice.

Moving forward like giant sheets of sandpaper, the ice ground down the rocks and gouged out deep valleys. When the ice melted, it left the debris scattered in a thick layer over the landscape.

But even the changes brought about by the Ice Age were small compared with what happened to the Earth earlier in its 4500 million year history (see opposite). The rocks tell a fantastic story of several generations of mountains being pushed up and worn down again. Even the land on which we live has been under the sea on many occasions as forces within the Earth caused the crust to buckle and bob up and down. These changes are still going on. They are generally extremely slow and we do not notice them but we are occasionally reminded of the Earth's instability when volcanoes erupt or earthquakes shatter the surface and transform it in minutes.

Vegetation and Soils

Heathland

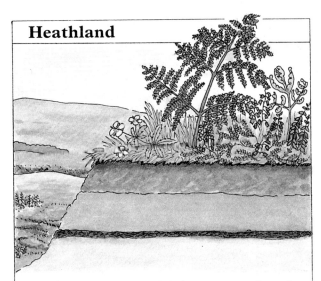

Heathland generally develops on sandy soils when the tree cover is removed. The vegetation consists of heathers, bracken and other plants that can survive in acidic soils. The soil is always in distinct layers and usually has a hard layer a little way below the surface.

Chalk Grassland

Chalk grassland may look natural but it is really the result of hundreds of years of grazing. The soil is thin but it supports many attractive flowers if the grazing is not too heavy. The landscape in an area of chalk rock usually consists of smoothly rounded hills.

Clay

Clay soils are rather soft and they are easily worn away by the weather. They tend to form wide, flat, lowland plains. Oak forest is the natural vegetation but most areas have been cleared of trees and are cultivated today. Powerful tractors are needed to pull ploughs through the heavy soil.

Limestone

Limestone rocks are rather hard and they form hilly regions with thin soils. When the vegetation is removed the soil is easily washed away, leaving bare limestone. Water gradually dissolves the rock, especially along the cracks, and forms structures such as the limestone pavement in the illustration above.

Vegetation and Soils

Vegetation and Landscape

Almost everywhere you go, whether in the hills or the lowlands, you will find the land covered with a living blanket of vegetation. The kinds of plant that grow in any one area depend on several factors. These include the climate, the underlying rocks and soil, and the use to which the land is put.

As you can see from the map below, most of Western Europe lies in the deciduous forest belt. The natural vegetation of this area is forest, which is made up of trees such as beech, oak, and ash. These deciduous trees all drop their leaves for the winter and flourish best where the climate is not too severe with rainfall well distributed throughout the year.

But relatively little of the original deciduous forest remains in Europe today. Over the last few thousand years people have cleared most forest land for their crops and grazing animals, which have changed the land still further. Much is now covered with grass. Naturalists carefully guard the remaining areas of original woodland as nature reserves to protect their rich plant and insect life.

On the opposite page you can see four very different scenes. Landscapes like these can be found in many parts of Europe; keep your eyes open for similar scenes on your travels. Three of the scenes look quite natural, but all have actually been created by human activity. All four areas were once wooded, but after the trees were cleared the soil determined the nature of the vegetation – and therefore the use to which the land could be put. This led to the four different scenes, which are of great interest to naturalists because of the different plants and animals they support.

Try to visit an area similar to one of those shown opposite. Use your notebook to record the general features of the landscape, together with details of the soil and the different kinds of plants and animals that you find. Try to visit the area at different times of the year and record the changes that you see. The most obvious changes are seasonal; notice how cereal crops turn from green to gold in the summer and how tree leaves change colour in the autumn. Record these changes in your notebook.

European Vegetation

The natural vegetation of Europe can be divided into four main regions: the treeless tundra of the far north; the northern coniferous forest or taiga; the deciduous forest and the dry evergreen forests of the Mediterranean area.

The deciduous forest belt is by far the largest region but most of the woodland has been cut down to make way for agriculture. Most of the Mediterranean forests of cork oaks and other evergreen trees have also largely been destroyed by the activities of people and grazing animals. Many of these areas are now covered with thick scrub called maquis. Many other parts, especially around the coast, have been built on. High mountains have their own vegetation, similar to the tundra, because they are so much colder than the surrounding lowlands.

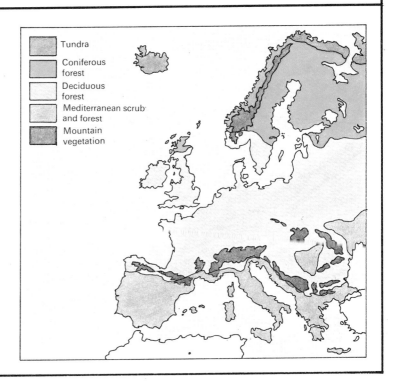

- Tundra
- Coniferous forest
- Deciduous forest
- Mediterranean scrub and forest
- Mountain vegetation

The Changing Landscape

Left: This scene at the Marseilles docks in France shows a completely artificial environment. Such areas are, of course, essential to modern life, but we could not live permanently in such a 'concrete jungle'. We must preserve large areas of the countryside if we are to survive.

Change and Conservation

Seasonal changes come round every year, but if you were able to study an area for several years you would see more permanent changes taking place in the vegetation and scenery. Bushes gradually invade grassland unless it is regularly cut or grazed, and ponds gradually disappear as they become choked with reeds and other plants. Even a river can change its course over the years as it seeks the easiest route down to the sea.

Try to find some old photographs or postcards in your local library to show you what your own area looked like about 100 years ago. The general landscape may look the same, and you might be able to recognize some of the buildings, but the vegetation will probably look rather different. Some of the changes may have come about naturally, but the greatest changes will have been brought about by people.

In some places the natural landscape and vegetation has been completely destroyed and replaced by the artificial landscape of towns and cities. With modern machinery such transformations can take place in a very short time. We need houses, roads, and factories, but we also need open spaces and wildlife. The nature conservation movement aims to ensure that we keep as much as possible of our wildlife for future generations, and we can do this only if we maintain the areas in which the plants and animals live. These areas are called

habitats. Oakwoods, chalk downs, heathlands, and seashores are all habitats. You will be able to think of many more, in water as well as on land. Each has a distinct set of physical conditions, such as climate and soil. Each also has its own collection of plants and animals that are suited to these conditions. If we destroy these habitats, the wildlife cannot survive.

The Ecosystem

When you begin to study the plants and animals of a particular habitat you are actually studying what biologists call an *ecosystem*. The plants and animals within the system have become suited to the physical conditions of the habitat. At the same time they have become adapted to each other and, over many generations, they have formed a very complex community. All the members of that community are linked together in a food web, such as the one shown in the diagram.

This is made up of many food chains and each chain consists of a plant and a small number of animal species. The plant is at the beginning of the chain, because only plants can make their own food. The first animal in the chain feeds on the plant and is in turn eaten by the second animal. And so it goes on, although you rarely find more than four or five different kinds of animal in the chain. The final one, known as the top predator, has no natural enemies.

Food Webs

A Food Web in a Meadow

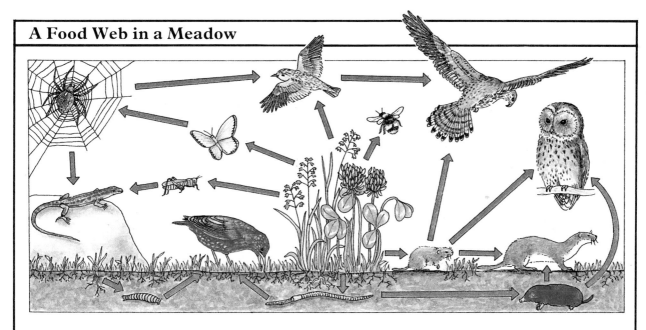

All life in a meadow depends ultimately on the grasses and other plants. Butterflies and bees sip nectar from the flowers, grasshoppers and voles eat the leaves, birds eat the seeds and worms eat the decaying roots. These animals are all herbivores ('plant-eaters') and they are in turn eaten by carnivores ('meat-eaters'). Follow the arrows to see who eats whom. Dead plants and animals and animal droppings are broken down to release nutrients into the soil. There they are taken up by plant roots to begin the cycle all over again.

Grass – Mouse – Fox is a very simple woodland food chain, with the fox being the top predator; in fact it is the only predator in this particular chain. You could equally well give Grass – Mouse – Owl as your simple food chain, because mice are eaten by owls as well as by foxes. And so, although foxes do not eat owls, they are linked together in the food web because both eat the same food. If the foxes ate all the mice, the owls would have to turn to other food or starve. In fact, of course, the foxes would not eat all the mice. If they ate too many and the mice became rare, the foxes themselves would have to turn to other food, which would allow the mouse population to build up again.

Most predators take several different kinds of prey, usually concentrating on the most easily available kind at any given season. They therefore belong to several different food chains. This is what makes the food web so complex and delicately balanced. The loss of any one kind of animal can completely change the balance, but as long as people do not interfere too much, the animals all regulate each other's numbers and the ecosystem maintains its long-term stability.

Detective Work

As you explore different habitats, such as woods and meadows, try to work out some of the food chains for yourself by watching what the various animals eat. What kinds of insect are caught and eaten by spiders? Does anything eat the spiders? It is not easy to see exactly what birds are eating in the trees, but if you shake a few branches over a sheet or an up-turned umbrella (see p.38) you might get a good idea of the sort of food available to the birds. Look for owl pellets (see p.21) to find out what the owls have been eating.

With this sort of detective work, you can work out many food chains and construct a simple food web for the area. You will discover many fascinating connections. For example, the number of cats in a village can

13

Food Webs

affect the amount of clover seed produced in the surrounding fields! The connection goes like this: clover seed develops only after bumble bees have pollinated the flowers; bumble bee nests are often attacked by field mice; cats catch field mice. The more cats there are, the fewer mice and the more bees – and therefore more clover seed. This amusing connection was first pointed out by the famous naturalist Charles Darwin in the 19th century. You could also say that the amount of clover seed depends on the number of owls, because owls also catch plenty of mice.

Studying the ecosystems and their food webs is fun, but it also has a serious purpose. Unless we know and understand the needs of the plants and animals around us, we cannot hope to maintain our countryside in a suitable condition for the wildlife. But why should we bother to keep all the different kinds of plants and animals? Surely, it would be a sad and empty world without the flowers and butterflies and birds, but it would also be an impossible world for us without wildlife. We belong to food webs just as much as the wild plants and animals do. It is certain that, in the long run, we could not survive without the natural world around us.

Right: The boulders on this mountain top have been produced by frost action. Rainwater gets into cracks in the rocks and, when it freezes, it expands with such force that the rocks split apart. The broken pieces gradually roll down the mountainside.

Below left: Rivers play a major role in shaping the land. This one is cutting its way through a field of volcanic rock in central Iceland.

Below right: Gardens are artificial environments but they are very important for wildlife because they provide several mini-habitats in a small area. Lawns, walls, flower beds and other parts of the garden all have plenty of animal life for you to watch.

Equipment

Be well prepared when you go out to explore the countryside. The weather can change rapidly, so make sure you have warm, waterproof clothing with you. Wear sensible, comfortable footwear (waterproof if you are going to wet places) and don't forget your notebook.

Keeping a Notebook

Your notebook is very important. Use it to note down everything you see and hear. Make sketches if you can and stick in things like leaves and feathers as well as photographs. Your notebook should be fun to read on winter evenings and it will tell you where to look for wildlife another time.

On Being A Naturalist

You must now be eager to get out and explore the countryside. The rest of this book deals with the different kinds of ecosystems that you may find around you – the woods, rivers, seashores, and so on. It should help you to identify and understand much of what you see. So how do you begin your study; how do you become a naturalist?

The naturalist watches – and watches and watches – so your most important asset is your eyes. You must learn how to look for things – for signs of animals as well as for the animals themselves – and then you must learn to watch. Every little detail of an animal's behaviour may be important, so you need the patience to watch for long periods. Your ears can also help you, especially if you are interested in birds, for the sounds of animals are very useful for locating and identifying the various species.

Remember that the animals themselves are very good at picking up sounds and will often hear you long before you can hear them. You must learn to walk quietly. A single twig cracking under your foot can startle a whole herd of deer and send them galloping away out of sight. Don't shout to your companions. Use a system of hand signals or soft whistles when you need to communicate from a distance. Most mammals also have a very good sense of smell and can pick up your scent from a considerable distance. Always try to approach with the wind blowing towards you so your scent is not blown towards the animals you are trying to watch.

What You Need

Human memory is never quite as good as you think it is. You cannot hope to be a good naturalist without a notebook – and don't forget your pencil! Note down everything you see and hear when watching wildlife; include details of the surroundings as well as the plants or animals you are studying. If it is an animal, try to note down all its movements and anything that it eats. If you are studying plants, make notes of any insects or other animals that visit or live on them. Your notes will help you to identify things when you get home, but it is a good idea to carry one or more pocket guides into the countryside with you so that you can identify things on the spot. A sturdy satchel, a rucksack or even a flight-bag is ideal for carrying your equipment.

Binoculars are obviously very useful for studying wildlife at a distance, and the bird-watcher will not get very far without them. You will find some tips for choosing binoculars on page 40. A lens or magnifying glass is essential for studying plants and insects because many of the things you have to look at are so small (see page 144). Most naturalists also like to take photographs of plants and animals and their habitats. You will find some information about wildlife photography on pages 145–147.

The kind of clothing that you wear will depend largely on the season and the weather. Remember, however, that a brilliant morning can deteriorate into a very wet afternoon, so be prepared for rain at all times. Don't wear bright colours if you are watching birds or mammals; try to wear something that will blend in with the surroundings and camouflage you. Take a plastic bag to sit on if you plan to watch in one place for any length of time. A bag is also useful for kneeling on to examine plants in damp places.

Don't go into the wilds alone, especially if you are planning to study lakes and rivers, and always tell your family where you are going.

Try to join your local natural history society or naturalists' trust. These organizations arrange visits to various habitats, including nature reserves, which you might not otherwise be able to visit. Many reserves and country parks now have nature trails to guide you through the area and to point out some of the more interesting features. As a member of a natural history society, you will also have the benefit of experienced naturalists to help you identify and understand what you see. With practice, you will be able to spot these things for yourself, and then you will really be a naturalist.

Nature Trails

Nature trails add much enjoyment to country walks by pointing out and explaining interesting features at certain points near the path. Here a well designed board enables visitors to identify the plants and animals they can see on and around a lake in a park.

The Country Code

Wildlife is precious. Don't do anything to damage it. Catching a few insects or other small animals for a closer look will do no harm as long as you remember to put them back where you found them. Always obey the *Country Code*.

1. Leave no litter.
2. Fasten all gates.
3. Avoid damaging fences, hedges and walls.
4. Guard against all fire risk.
5. Keep dogs under control.
6. Keep to paths across farmland.
7. Safeguard all water supplies.
8. Protect all forms of wildlife.
9. Go carefully on country roads.
10. Respect the life of the countryside.

WOODLANDS

When the ice retreated from Europe at the end of the
Ice Age, forests gradually spread over the land. Only
the northern tundra and the highest mountains
remained without a covering of trees. Over the last
5000 years, people have cut down most of the original
forests to make way for agriculture, but most areas still
have small areas of woodland for you to explore.

Take a walk through the woodlands in your area and
discover the fascinating wildlife of these shady places.
Learn to recognize the trees and other plants that make
up the various levels within the wood. Find out how to
tell the age of a tree and uncover some of the secrets of
life on the woodland floor.

A Woodland Walk

The well-worn woodland path emerges into a large clearing where fallow deer graze peacefully. Their eyes and ears are always alert for danger and the animals bolt for the safety of the trees as you approach. A jay and a chaffinch fly off noisily too, but the coal tit calmly goes on picking insects from the oak leaves. The large oaks at the edge of the clearing show signs of age: branches are dying and many have already fallen. Large bracket fungi, such as the dryad's saddle, grow on the trunks and weaken them still further. Many smaller bracket fungi grow on the dead stumps.

The woodland margin supports a fantastic variety of wildlife. The extra light at the edge of the wood encourages the growth of many more small plants than you will see in the shadowy centre. Flowers bloom throughout the spring and summer. Tree seedlings also sprout in the clearings but the deer give them little chance to grow. Deer don't like bracken, however, so this tall fern may spread rapidly. Hordes of insects enjoy the rich plant life. Butterflies sun themselves on the leaves and feed at the flowers. Hornets make their homes in hollow trees, while stag beetles and many others breed in the decaying stumps.

As you walk on down the path into the trees the ground gets damper. Clumps of male fern, looking like huge green shuttlecocks, replace the bracken and there are fewer flowers on the ground. A small stream trickles out of sight through the wood at the bottom of the slope. Many woodland animals come here to drink, leaving footprints for you to identify.

Beyond the stream the path rises up and skirts a pine plantation. The original oak woodland has been cut down to make way for the quick-growing conifers which provide much of our timber today. Sections of the plantation have recently been cleared and replanted with young trees. For a few years

the young plantations are like woodland clearings with large numbers of flowers, insects and birds. Voles are also very common and often damage many of the young trees. The kestrel enjoys hunting here and is a good friend of the forester. The conifers are planted close together and as they grow they gradually cut out the light from the ground. Few plants can grow then and the animals are driven out. As you walk by the plantation you can see how dark it is. Even the lower branches are dead because there is no light.

The different types of woodland each have their own plants and animals for you to explore. Look carefully around you, and take a notebook in which to record your observations. A hand lens (x 10 is a good size) will also be useful for detailed examinations and a pair of binoculars (see page 40) for watching birds and mammals from a distance.

Woodland Types

The woodlands of Europe are of two main kinds – deciduous and evergreen. The deciduous trees drop their leaves in the autumn, but evergreens remain green throughout the year. Evergreen woods consist mainly of cone-bearing trees and most are found in colder regions – in the north and on the mountains. Deciduous forests contain different kinds of trees, but one kind is generally dominant. Look at your local woods and find out the kind of tree that occurs most. The kinds of trees growing in a wood depend largely on the type of soil.

Right: Beech trees cast deep shade and few plants can grow below them. Here a beech seedling is shooting up where a shaft of sunlight reaches the forest floor. One day it may grow large enough to replace one of the old trees of the forest. But very few seedlings ever get to this stage.

Above: Oak trees let plenty of light through to the woodland floor, even in summer, allowing bracken and many other plants to flourish.

An Oakwood

Most people can recognize oak trees by their leaves and their acorns, but did you know that we have two common species of oak? The pedunculate oak has stalked acorn cups and almost stalkless leaves, while the sessile oak has stalkless acorn cups and long stalks on its leaves. If you have oakwoods near your home, work out which kind of oak forms it. If you live in an upland area with relatively shallow soil you will probably find that the sessile oak is dominant. The pedunculate oak prefers to grow in the deeper soils of the valleys and the lowlands and is especially common on heavy clay. You can find both oaks together in many woods.

Oak trees come into leaf quite late in the spring, and even when in full leaf they do not cast a very deep shade. Lots of small plants can grow beneath them, especially on the deep rich soils of the pedunculate oakwoods. Some of the familiar flowers are shown on pages 34 and 35. Hazel grows everywhere in many oakwoods. It used to be cut to the ground every few years to provide slender poles for beansticks and hurdle-making. This system, known as coppicing, is still used in some woods, especially in nature reserves. It encourages flowering plants to spread over the ground, and the young stems sprouting from the cut stumps of the trees and shrubs provide plenty of cover for birds.

Ash trees are common in many oakwoods. They used to be coppiced like the hazel, and still are in some places. Their young trunks make excellent tool handles. Look for ash trees with several trunks rising up from a single base. These are trees which have been coppiced in the past and then allowed to grow up from the stumps. Pure ashwoods grow in some limestone districts.

A Beechwood

Beech trees, recognized by their very smooth bark and pointed buds (see page 22), like well-drained soils. The largest beechwoods in Britain are on the chalky and sandy soils of the south and east. Beech trees cast a very deep shade and few plants can survive underneath them. There might be drifts of bluebells in the spring, flowering and making their food before the beech leaves are fully open, but in the summer there is little but a thick layer of dead beech leaves. It is very much easier to walk through a beechwood than an oakwood.

Above: A natural pine forest in Scotland. Notice the well spaced trees. Plenty of light reaches through and allows heather to grow thickly below.

A Pinewood

You will have to go to northern regions or to the mountains to see natural pinewoods. The Scots pine is the commonest species. Look for the brick-red bark on its upper parts. It forms huge forests in parts of Scandinavia. Natural

Examining Owl Pellets

Owls swallow their prey whole, but they can't digest the fur and bones. When the flesh has been digested, the fur and bones are formed into a sausage-shaped pellet which is coughed up and spat out. Owls may produce two or three pellets in a day. Look for them under trees. Large numbers of pellets pile up under regular roosting places. The pellets are not smelly and if you pull them to pieces you can see what the owl has been eating. Stick the bones on a card and try to work out what parts of the body they came from. The triangular shoulder blades are easily identified. The prey animals are best identified by their skulls and jaws. Shrew teeth are sharply pointed and often tipped with red. Voles have long, chisel-like front teeth and a flat-topped wall of grinding teeth further back. Mouse skulls are similar, but the grinding teeth have more rounded surfaces. You can clean up the bones with the aid of tweezers and then bleach them by leaving them in hydrogen peroxide.

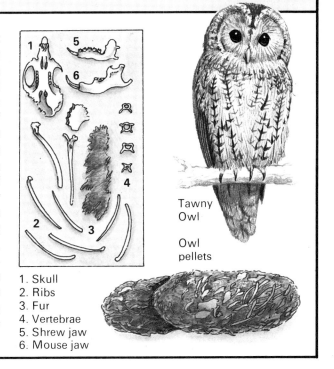

Tawny Owl

Owl pellets

1. Skull
2. Ribs
3. Fur
4. Vertebrae
5. Shrew jaw
6. Mouse jaw

Identifying Trees

Turkey

Red

Holm

Pedunculate

Oak

Beech

Hornbeam

Alder

Field Maple

Ash

Small-leaved Lime

Sycamore

Hazel

Horse Chestnut

Hawthorn

Wild Cherry

Larch

Norway Spruce

Wych Elm

Silver Birch

Sweet Chestnut

False Acacia

Holly

Scots Pine

Yew

pinewoods are often quite open, with carpets of heather and bilberry bushes beneath the trees and birch trees mixed with them. The ground is covered with fungi in the autumn.

Other common cone-bearing trees include the spruces, with their long, sausage-shaped cones, and the larches. The latter are unusual conifers in that they drop their leaves in the autumn.

Identify the Trees

Some of the commoner woodland trees are illustrated here. Learning their leaf shapes is one of the best ways to identify them in the woods. The flowers and fruits are also very helpful, although they are not always present. Bark patterns will help you to recognize some species. The wild cherry, for example, is easily identified by its horizontal stripes and by the way in which the young bark flakes off in horizontal bands. The sweet chestnut has a spiral pattern on the lower part of the trunk. Look out, too, for the silvery bark and black triangles of the silver birch.

Examine the winter buds of deciduous trees. Their shapes and colours will help with

Grow a Horse Chestnut Bud

The winter buds of deciduous trees contain the next year's leaves, well wrapped up against the cold winds. The leaves start to expand and the buds burst open when the sap rises in the spring. Put a few twigs in water in early spring and watch the leaves unfold. It is best to use a large-leaved species like the horse chestnut seen here.

Bud

Leaf scar

23

Tree Projects

Finding the Height of a Tree

Two simple methods of estimating the height of a tree (or a building) are shown below.

Method 1: For this method you will need the help of a friend. Hold a ruler or a straight stick vertically in front of you and walk backwards or forwards until the stick appears to be exactly the same size as the tree: the bottom of the stick should coincide with the base of the tree and the top should appear level with the top of the tree. Keep your arm in the same position and swivel the stick until it is horizontal. Keep one end lined up with the base of the tree and ask your friend to walk along until he or she appears to be at the other end of the stick. Shout 'stop!' The distance from your friend to the base of the tree should equal the height of the tree.

Method 2: You can carry out this method by yourself. All you need is a straight stick *the same length* as the distance from your eye to your outstretched hand. Hold the stick upright at arm's length and move backwards or forwards until the stick coincides with the tree as in the first method. The distance from you to the base of the tree is then the same as the height of the tree. Pace out the distance or measure it with a long measuring tape.

You can test the accuracy of your measurements by testing these methods on a church tower or similar building of known height. Make a note of the tallest tree you can find. What kind is it? Did you know that some redwood trees in California are over 100 metres high?

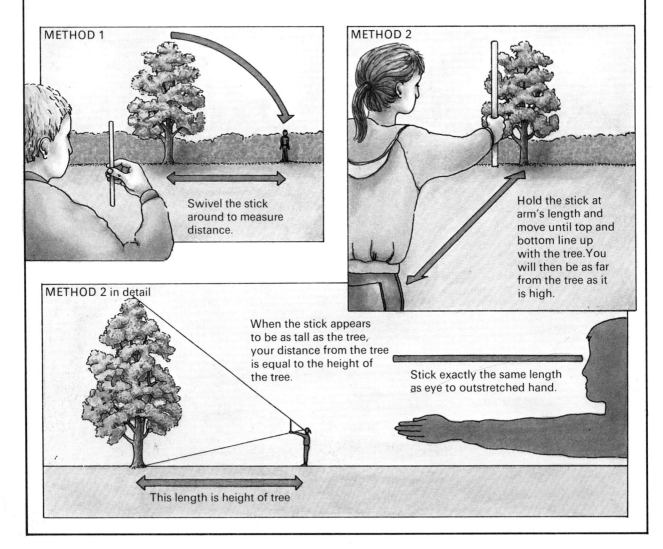

METHOD 1

Swivel the stick around to measure distance.

METHOD 2

Hold the stick at arm's length and move until top and bottom line up with the tree. You will then be as far from the tree as it is high.

METHOD 2 in detail

When the stick appears to be as tall as the tree, your distance from the tree is equal to the height of the tree.

Stick exactly the same length as eye to outstretched hand.

This length is height of tree

Tree Projects

Trees from Twigs

Small pieces of twig, known as cuttings, often grow roots if stuck in the soil, or even in a jar of water. Take cuttings from various trees and see which root most easily. Poplars and willows are very quick. Hawthorn is also a good tree to try. It is often better to pull off a shoot with a 'heel' than to cut it off.

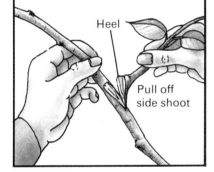

Heel

Pull off side shoot

Making Bark Rubbings

Look at the trunks of different kinds of trees and see how the bark patterns vary. Make a collection of the patterns by taking bark rubbings. You need some large sheets of fairly tough paper and a thick wax crayon. Some string may be useful for holding the paper on the tree, but a friend is better! Make sure that the paper can't move and then rub the crayon firmly over it. Watch how the bark pattern appears on the paper. Label the pattern with the name of the tree and keep it in your natural history collection. Fix one of the tree's leaves to the paper as well if you like.

The Age of a Tree

Find a tree that has recently been cut down and look at the pattern of rings on the cut surface. Count the number of rings as carefully as you can: it is not always easy when you get close to the centre. Each ring of wood was formed during one year of the tree's growth, so by counting these annual rings you can tell how old the tree was when it was felled. Trees growing by themselves – in parks, for example – grow more quickly than trees in the woods because they have no competition. Their annual rings are broader than those of woodland trees. Notice the shoots already springing from the stump just a few months after it was cut.

Flowers, Fruits and Seeds

identification. Some of the easiest to recognize are the sharply pointed buds of the beech and the velvety black buds of the ash. Look at the twigs as well and see whether there are any little scars showing where the previous year's leaves fell. These scars are very obvious in the horse chestnut.

Tree Reproduction

Apart from the pines and other conifers, all our trees produce flowers. But not all the flowers are as obvious as those of the horse chestnut below. They often have no petals and no scent and they are pollinated by the wind. The hazel is a good example. Look for its long yellow catkins scattering pollen very

From Flower to Fruit

The horse chestnut originally came from Greece and is more common in parks and gardens than in woods. It is planted for its beautiful flowers (right). These are pollinated by bumble bees (below). After pollination the pistil of each flower swells to

Horse Chestnut flowers

Pistil

Stamen

form the familiar prickly green fruit (below right). The fruit dries and splits when it is ripe to reveal the shiny brown seed that we call a conker. There are sometimes two conkers in each fruit. These large seeds have no special mechanism for dispersal.

Plant a fresh conker in a flower pot filled with rich soil. Keep it moist and you will soon see the seedling horse chestnut tree appear.

Fruit

Seed

Seeds and Fruits

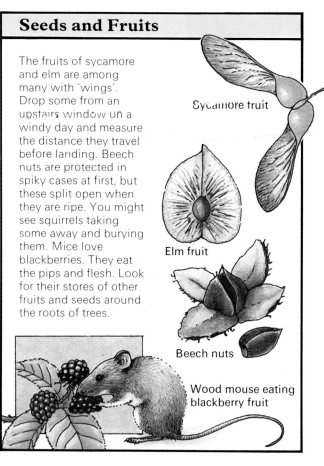

The fruits of sycamore and elm are among many with 'wings'. Drop some from an upstairs window on a windy day and measure the distance they travel before landing. Beech nuts are protected in spiky cases at first, but these split open when they are ripe. You might see squirrels taking some away and burying them. Mice love blackberries. They eat the pips and flesh. Look for their stores of other fruits and seeds around the roots of trees.

Sycamore fruit

Elm fruit

Beech nuts

Wood mouse eating blackberry fruit

early in the spring, long before the leaves open. The catkins consist only of male flowers. The female flowers, which are the ones that produce the nuts, look just like buds, but if you look carefully you will see tiny tufts of red hairs at the tip. These tufts are the stigmas, waiting to catch the pollen drifting in the breeze.

The ash and the elm also flower before their leaves open. Oak and beech produce their catkins at the same time as the leaves. Look for the flowers on other woodland trees and make drawings of them in your notebook.

Seed Dispersal

When the flowers have been pollinated they begin to swell up and form the fruits. The seeds develop inside the fruits. When the fruits and their seeds are ripe they are dispersed or scattered by the wind or by various animals. In this way the seeds get distributed over a wide area and some of them get a chance to grow into new trees. Look for seedling trees in the woods. They crop up all over the place, but you will notice that they never grow very big if they are under mature trees. Only those that spring up in a clearing – perhaps where an old tree has fallen – can grow properly. Eventually one outgrows the others and replaces the tree that fell.

Fleshy or juicy fruits, like cherries and crab apples, attract birds and other animals. The fruit is eaten, but the hard seeds are often spat out to grow where they fall. Some seeds are, of course, swallowed with the fleshy bit of the fruit, but this doesn't always mean that they are destroyed. Many pass right through the animals, and they often germinate even better after this treatment. Hard fruits, such as hazel nuts and acorns, attract squirrels and other animals who crack the shells to get at the seeds inside. They eat thousands of seeds and this might seem rather wasteful for the trees. But remember that the animals bury a lot of nuts as well, and they don't always remember where these stores are. Some of the buried seeds can then grow into new trees. A tree may produce many thousands of seeds during its life, and only one has to survive to replace the parent tree one day. Gather as many different woodland fruits as you can. Examine them to work out how each is dispersed and to find out what animals, if any, are involved in scattering each species.

Woodland Layers

A mature woodland of oak or ash has four fairly distinct layers. The trees themselves form the top layer, which is known as the canopy. Try to work out the height of the canopy when exploring the woodlands – see page 24. The shrub layer comes next. It includes hawthorn, blackthorn, hazel, holly and many other species. This layer is especially thick near the edge of the wood where there is more light. Underneath the shrub layer comes the field layer, consisting of the ferns and numerous flowering plants. Most of the flowers, such as violets and primroses, appear early in the year before the trees blot out too much light. The lowest

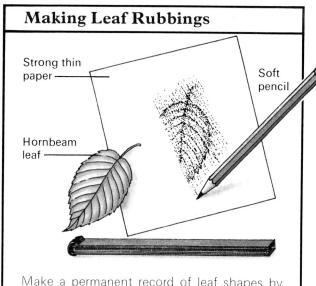

Making Leaf Rubbings

Strong thin paper

Soft pencil

Hornbeam leaf

Make a permanent record of leaf shapes by leaf-rubbing. Pick a fresh, unchewed leaf and cover it with a clean sheet of paper. Holding it firmly in place, rub over the whole leaf area with a soft pencil. The shape of the leaf and its veins is transferred to the paper. You could use a green pencil for a natural effect – or browns and yellows for autumn colours. Label the rubbing with the name of the tree and paste it into your notebook.

woodland layer is the ground layer which contains the mosses and liverworts and large numbers of toadstools. But the most important component of the ground layer is its carpet of dead leaves. Each of the four layers supports its own collection of animals, although some of the larger animals regularly move from one layer to another.

A Continuous Cycle

The leaves that fall in autumn are soon attacked by fungi and they start to rot. Collect a handful of dead leaves from the woodland floor and look for the branching white threads of the fungi. They grow all over the leaves and take food from them. The leaves gradually crumble away, and as they decay they give minerals back to the soil. More minerals are released when the fungi die. The minerals can be taken up by the roots of the trees and other plants and in this way there is a continuous recycling of the woodland material – from soil

The Woodland Floor

Above: These tawny grisette toadstools, forcing their way through the mosses and leaf litter, have sprung from a huge network of fungal threads – part of the complex living community of the woodland floor.

to tree, to soil again. Dead wood is recycled in just the same way.

Although fungi are very important in the breakdown of woodland materials, many other organisms are involved as well. Microscopic bacteria play a big part, and so do the hordes of insects and mites that live and feed among the leaf litter.

Autumn Toadstools

The fungal threads that you see spreading through the dead leaves are mostly the early stages of toadstools. They spend most of the year soaking up food from the leaves, and when they have absorbed enough they form the toadstools, which are their reproductive bodies. Look under some toadstools and you will find either lots of gills, spreading out like the spokes of a wheel, or a spongy surface with thousands of tiny pores. The gills and the

Making Spore Prints

Mushroom cap —

Card —
Print of the spores —

To get some idea of the vast numbers of spores scattered by toadstools, lay a cap on a piece of paper and leave it for a few hours. Lift it carefully to see the spore print where millions of tiny spores have fallen on to the paper. It is best to cover the cap with a basin while the print is being made because the slightest draught can disturb the spore pattern. Use dark paper for white-spored species.

WOODLAND FUNGI
**NEVER EXPERIMENT
WITH EATING
WILD FUNGI**

Chanterelle

Plums and Custard

Fly Agaric
POISONOUS

Earth Star

Crumble Cap

Amethyst Deceiver

Honey Fungus

Sickener
POISONOUS

Blusher

Cep

Death Cap
DEADLY POISONOUS

Bracket Fungus

Common Puffball

linings of the pores produce millions of minute spores which blow away in the wind. If they fall in suitable places they grow into new threads to start the sequence all over again. Look for earthstars and club-shaped puffballs. These fungi throw out their spores when disturbed. Drop a small twig on to one and watch the spores come out like a puff of smoke.

The Life of the Wood Ant

If you visit pinewoods or relatively dry oakwoods between spring and late autumn you might well meet the wood ants. These large reddish brown ants build huge nest mounds with pine needles and other plant debris. Many thousands of ants live in a single nest, and if you keep very quiet you can actually hear them rustling the dead leaves as they scurry over the woodland floor.

Wood ants don't sting, but they will bite and squirt formic acid at you if you annoy them. If you wear wellington boots and spray these with a good insect repellent, you can get right up to the nest and the ants won't bother you. Watch the army of worker ants bringing

The Quick-growing Stinkhorn

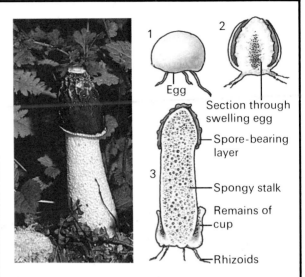

1 Egg
2 Section through swelling egg
Spore-bearing layer
3 Spongy stalk
Remains of cup
Rhizoids

You will smell the stinkhorn in the woods long before you see this strange toadstool. Starting from the 'egg' stage, the spongy spike can grow to 15 centimetres in an hour. A fresh stinkhorn has a slimy cap covered with spores. Flies are attracted by the smell and feed on the slime. They pick up spores on their feet and carry them off to grow elsewhere.

The Wood Ants

Wood ant nests are often built around old tree stumps (below). The mound containing many tunnels and chambers is made largely of plant debris, but the ants hate 'foreign' material. Put some cocktail sticks on to a mound and watch the ants drag them away (right).

CROSS-SECTION OF A NEST

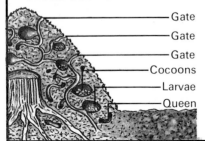

Gate
Gate
Gate
Cocoons
Larvae
Queen

food to the nest. All kinds of insects are dragged along – if they are too heavy the ants cut them up first. Many of the insects are caught in the trees and foresters like to have the ants around because they destroy so many pests. In some countries the wood ants are protected by law for this reason. As well as insects, the ants collect lots of honeydew which oozes out of aphids. It has been estimated that the workers of a large colony may collect 50 kilogrammes of honeydew in one summer. Watch the ants bring building materials to the mound and tug them right to the top. But they won't thank you for helping them: any material that you throw on will be immediately dragged down again and hauled right away from the nest.

The mound is only part of the nest. There are many chambers and tunnels right under the ground. Many queens live here, busily laying eggs throughout the summer. The workers feed the grubs here as well. Mating flights take place in early summer, with most of the new queens returning to their own nests after mating. The ants all hibernate for the winter in the deepest part of the nest. The

mound sinks at this time of the year and has to be rebuilt in the spring.

Life in the Leaf Litter

The leaf litter that covers the woodland floor provides food and shelter for an astonishing variety of small animals. Two ways of finding these creatures – the pitfall trap and the Tullgren funnel – are described below. An even simpler method is to spread a handful of moist leaf litter over a large sheet of paper and search through it with a lens. A torch will help if you actually do this in the woods. Count the number of animals you can find in a handful of litter. For every one you find there will be many more that you don't see, for many of the animals are extremely tiny.

The springtails are usually the most noticeable creatures in this miniature world because they get very agitated and leap all over the place when disturbed. They are primitive wingless insects which feed on decaying leaves. With your lens, you might just be able to make out a forked spring at the hind end. When released by the springtail, it flicks the insect forwards. Look for mites as

Make a Pitfall Trap

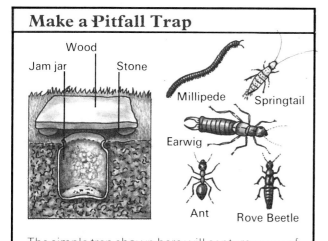

The simple trap shown here will capture many of the small creatures that roam the woodland floor at night. Make sure that the rim of the jar is absolutely level with the ground, and then the animals will crawl straight in. The cover keeps out the rain. Empty the trap in the morning. Some of the commonly captured animals are shown here.

The Tullgren Funnel

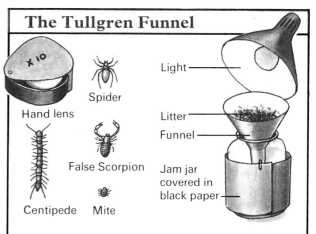

Many minute animals live in moist leaf litter. You can find them with the apparatus shown here. Put some litter in the funnel and shine the light on it for a few hours. To avoid the heat and the dryness the animals burrow deeper into the litter. Many fall into the jar below. Line it with some damp blotting paper to keep them alive until you can examine them with a hand lens.

Mosses and Liverworts

well. Globular ones with spiky legs are very common. They feed by sucking the juices from decaying leaves and from fungal threads. The red velvet mites are carnivorous, but the most fascinating of the predatory creatures in the leaf litter are the false scorpions. Far too small to harm us, they use their pink claws to catch and poison mites and other tiny prey.

Mosses and Liverworts

These small flowerless plants generally grow in damp places and often form thick cushions or mats on the woodland floor. In really damp woods they even grow on the trees. Mosses have both slender creeping stems and short upright ones, clothed with very small leaves. Their cushion-like and mat-like growth helps to hold moisture around the delicate leaves. At certain times of the year they send out slender stalks topped by spore capsules that look like miniature pepper-pots. Spores are

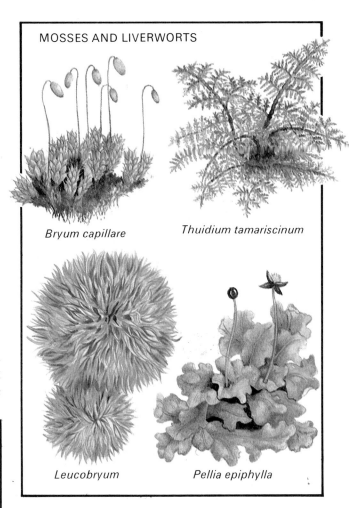

MOSSES AND LIVERWORTS

Bryum capillare

Thuidium tamariscinum

Leucobryum

Pellia epiphylla

Investigate a Moss

Use your lens to examine moss spore capsules. Each has a sort of pixie-hood at first, but this falls as the capsule ripens. Look at the end of a ripe capsule. It is like a tiny pepper-pot. Notice the tiny holes through which the minute spores escape. They open in dry weather and close in the wet.

Ripe capsule with hood about to fall

Open capsule (spores dispersed)

Stalk

Swan-necked Thread Moss

scattered in dry weather and those that reach suitably moist places will grow into new mosses. You can grow some yourself by shaking ripe capsules over some damp peat in a plastic box. Keep the box closed and the spores will soon produce a mat of greenish threads from which the mosses will sprout.

There are many different kinds of mosses. The fern-like *Thuidium* (above) is easy to recognize, and you should be able to pick out the greyish green spongy cushions of *Leucobryum* on the woodland floor. The bright green capsules help to identify *Bryum capillare*. Other mosses may not be as easy to identify. You will need a good lens to look at the shapes of their leaves and the help of detailed guide books.

Liverworts like even damper places than mosses. Many of them look just like mosses, but they have much simpler spore capsules that split right open and look like stars when they are ripe. But some liverworts look more like seaweeds. Look for these on the banks of shady woodland streams. *Pellia* (left) is a very common example. Lift up a piece and see the very simple roots that anchor it to the ground. Some liverworts carry little cups full of detachable buds. Raindrops falling into the cups splash the buds out and each can grow into a new plant.

The Field Layer

Flowering plants and ferns make up the woodland field layer. Most of the plants are soft-stemmed herbaceous species that die down in the autumn and send up new shoots in the spring. Many of the flowers grow from underground bulbs or tubers – a well-known bulbous species is the bluebell.

Like the shrub layer, the field layer is poorly developed in beechwoods and other dense woodlands and it is not found at all in mature conifer plantations. It reaches its greatest development in lightly grazed woodland clearings and places where trees have fallen and light is let in. There is also a very rich field layer in the woods which are regularly coppiced (see page 20). There are always some open areas in coppiced woodland in which flowers can flourish. As the new

Below: Foxgloves grow tall in an overgrown woodland clearing with elder bushes in flower behind them. Both of these plants spring up rapidly when trees are felled.

Woodland Flowers

coppice shoots grow up and shade the field layer some plants die, but others remain 'ticking over' without flowering until the coppice is cut some years later. After a year of sunlight, during which they build up food reserves, the plants flower again in profusion.

The kinds of flowers that grow in the field layer depend very much on the type of soil and the amount of moisture it holds. In pedunculate oakwoods, for example, where the soil is deep and rich, you could find bugle, primroses, yellow archangel, woodruff and early purple orchids, together with large patches of dog's mercury in which very little else can grow. The dog's mercury is a dark green plant, up to about 40 centimetres high, with inconspicuous spikes of greenish flowers in spring. You might mistake it for stinging nettles at first, but its leaves are smoother and more rounded. Dog's mercury tolerates shade reasonably well and can actually grow under beeches if they are not too dense. As the leaves of the trees grow and cast more shade, the dog's mercury leaves produce more chlorophyll and become darker. This helps them to make the best use of the available light. Many other field layer plants darken in this way during the summer.

The field layer of a sessile oakwood generally has fewer species than that of the pedunculate oakwood because the soil is shallower and not so rich. Common species include foxglove, wood sorrel and common cow-wheat. The latter is able to tolerate more shade than most plants and actually puts out its flowers, looking like spindly yellow snapdragons, in the middle of summer when the woodland canopy is at its densest. Bluebells also thrive on the shallow soils, but they don't like shade and they die down by mid-summer, after storing up most of the food that they need for the next spring.

Use a good guide book to help you to identify the flowers that you find in the woodlands. Write their names in your notebook and make a note of the kinds of woods in which you found them and the time of year. What is the soil like? You will find that most plants have definite preferences

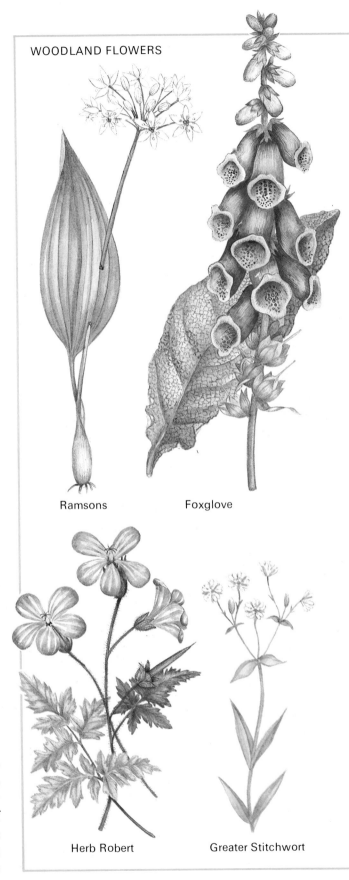

WOODLAND FLOWERS

Ramsons   Foxglove

Herb Robert   Greater Stitchwort

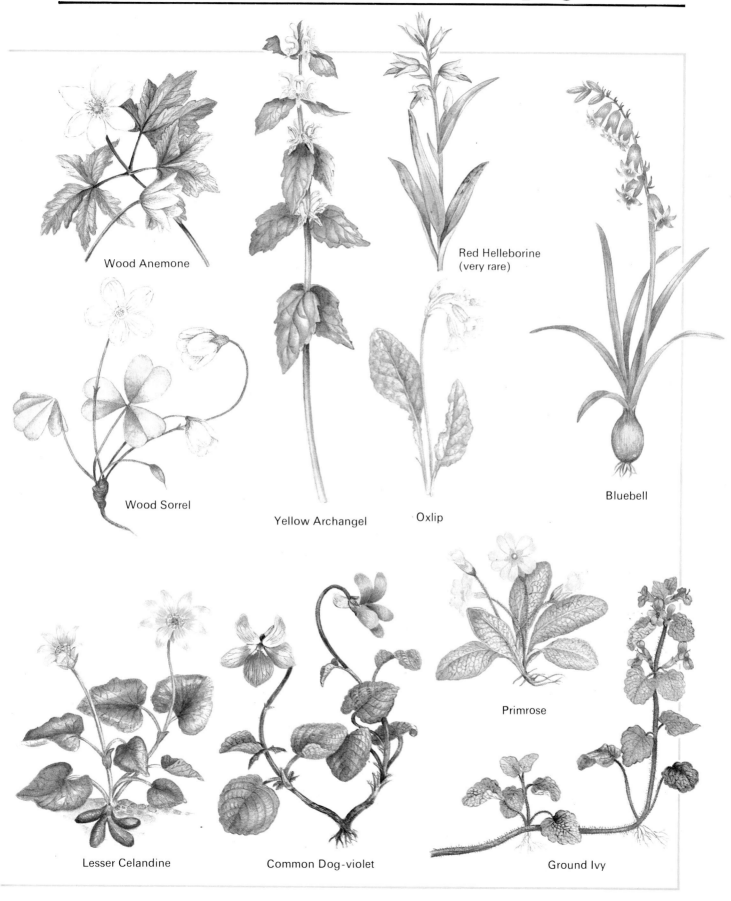

Wood Anemone

Wood Sorrel

Yellow Archangel

Red Helleborine (very rare)

Oxlip

Bluebell

Lesser Celandine

Common Dog-violet

Primrose

Ground Ivy

Ferns

regarding the soil, but some occur in all kinds of woodlands. The wood anemone and herb robert are among these wide-ranging species.

Have a look at the brambles in the woods. Although they can use their hooked prickles to scramble over other shrubs, they often form thick carpets on the woodland floor and can be taken as part of the field layer. Notice how the tips of the branches take root when they touch the ground. The plants don't flower much when growing in the wood in this way, so don't expect to find many blackberries.

Woodland Ferns

Ferns all need damp conditions to reproduce themselves and are much commoner in western regions of the British Isles, where rainfall is heavy, than in the east. In the wettest areas they often grow on the branches of the trees. The common polypody (opposite) is the commonest of our epiphytic or tree-growing ferns.

The male fern, pictured below, is often found on the woodland floor wherever conditions are reasonably damp. It has a short underground stem which sends up a cluster of

The Bird's Nest Orchid

The bird's nest orchid is one of a number of strange woodland flowers with no green colouring and no leaves. It can't make food in the normal way. Instead it absorbs ready-made food from dead and decaying leaves on the woodland floor. Because it does not need sunlight, this orchid can grow in very dark woods. Look for it in beech woods from May to July. It is one of the few flowering plants that can survive in the deep shade under the beeches. Even the flowers have no bright colour, but they smell quite sweetly of honey which attracts various small flies. The plant gets its name from its tangled cluster of roots, which resemble a small nest.

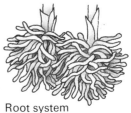

Root system

Growing Ferns from Spores

Look under fern fronds for the clusters of brown spore capsules. Those shown below belong to the male fern. Scatter some spores over moist sand or peat in a plastic box. Keep it covered and watch how the spores grow. They develop into heart-shaped plates called prothalli, and new ferns later grow from these. You will need your lens to look at the prothalli.

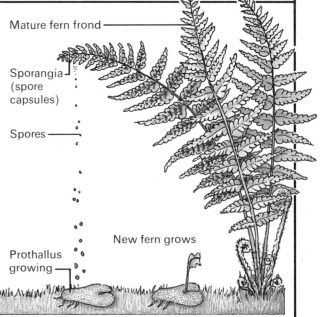

Mature fern frond

Sporangia (spore capsules)

Spores

New fern grows

Prothallus growing

large green leaves each spring. Notice how the leaves or fronds unfurl. This is typical of ferns, but not seen in any other group of plants. Look closely at the base of the fern and you will see the next year's leaves already tightly coiled there. Each leaf is divided into numerous small leaflets.

Ferns have no flowers and they reproduce by means of minute spores. If you brush against a fern in summer you might well find yourself covered with the powdery brown spores. Look under the fronds to see the clusters of spore capsules which release the spores. The capsules are arranged in different ways in different ferns.

The commonest fern is the bracken. This tall species has more or less triangular fronds which arise singly instead of in clusters as in the male fern and most other ferns. The young fronds look like little shepherds' crooks when they first push through the ground. This curving of the shoot protects the very delicate tissues at the tip. Bracken does not rely entirely on its spores for its spread and can thrive in much drier places than other ferns. It has a creeping underground stem that can extend more than a metre a year. The plant covers the ground in many sessile oakwoods and pinewoods and also spreads over huge areas of heathland. If you see it in the woods you can be sure that the soil is well drained, for the bracken cannot survive having its roots in water for long.

Look for other kinds of ferns on rocky woodland banks. Three common species are shown on the right. The hard fern carries its spores on special upright fronds which die when the spores have blown away. The hart's tongue doesn't look like a fern at all until you see the spore capsules under the leaves.

Woodland Insects

Examine any ten leaves from woodland trees and other plants in the summer: at least seven will probably show signs of insect attack. Holes in the middle suggest that they have been nibbled by beetles, while bits taken from the edges may be the work of beetles or caterpillars. Look under the leaves for aphids.

COMMON FERNS

Hart's Tongue Fern

Common Polypody

Hard Fern

The Marble Gall

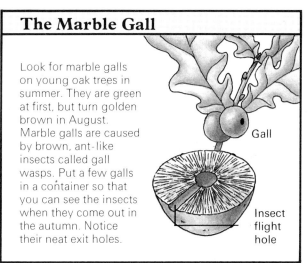

Look for marble galls on young oak trees in summer. They are green at first, but turn golden brown in August. Marble galls are caused by brown, ant-like insects called gall wasps. Put a few galls in a container so that you can see the insects when they come out in the autumn. Notice their neat exit holes.

Gall

Insect flight hole

Butterflies and Moths

Use a Beating Tray

A sharp knock will send lots of insects tumbling from the branches of trees and shrubs. You can catch them in a simple beating tray, made from part of an old sheet stretched over a light wooden frame or you can just lay a sheet on the ground. Keep a note of the insects you get from each kind of tree before releasing them. The yellow-tail caterpillar (below) is often beaten from hawthorn in the spring.

Pale blotches may show where minute grubs have burrowed between the upper and lower leaf surfaces. The burrows are called leaf mines. Look for the long twisting mines on bramble leaves, excavated by the caterpillars of a tiny moth.

Keep your eyes open for plant galls as well. These strange growths are especially common on oak trees. There are many different kinds, each caused by a different kind of insect. But it is not just the leaves that are attacked: flowers and fruits and even the timber itself all provide food for insects. And then there are the many carnivorous insects in the wood, including the ladybirds and many other beetles. Look out for the delicate green lacewings which fly from many plants when disturbed. You might startle the oak bush-cricket, a pale green grasshopper-like insect that rests in the trees by day. It feeds on small caterpillars and other insects.

Moths and Butterflies

Moths generally fly at night and rest by day. Search the tree trunks for resting moths. Many are very well camouflaged to protect them from birds. Others prefer to hide amongst the leaves. Some woodland moths are pictured below. The speckled yellow and

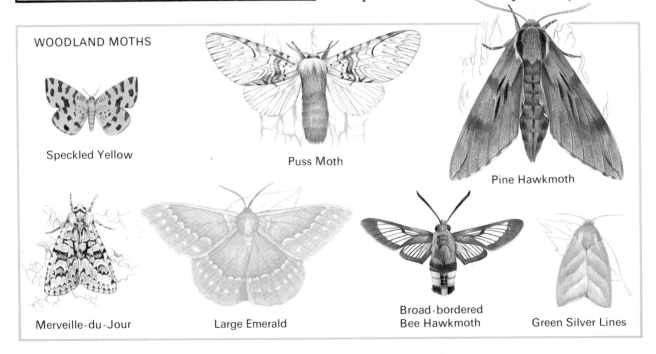

WOODLAND MOTHS

Speckled Yellow

Puss Moth

Pine Hawkmoth

Merveille-du-Jour

Large Emerald

Broad-bordered Bee Hawkmoth

Green Silver Lines

the broad-bordered bee hawkmoth fly in woodland clearings in the sunshine, but the others are nocturnal.

Butterflies are sun-loving insects and you must look for the woodland species in rides and clearings. They enjoy sunbathing on the leaves. Most of them take nectar from flowers, but the purple emperor prefers to drink honeydew deposited on the leaves by aphids. This striking butterfly spends most of its time flying around tall oak trees, although it sometimes comes down to drink from muddy pools and also has a liking for rotting meat. Collectors used to lure the butterfly to the ground by putting down a dead rabbit or other flesh.

WOODLAND BUTTERFLIES

Pearl-bordered Fritillary

male

British form

Southern European form

Speckled Wood

caterpillar

female

Silver-washed Fritillary

Ringlet

Purple Emperor

Lesser Purple Emperor (not found in Britain)

caterpillar

White Admiral

Woodland Birds

Woodland Birds

The birds are the most obvious of the woodland animals. You can't go into a wood without hearing them, even if you can't see them right away. A few of the many different kinds of woodland birds are pictured opposite. Some, like the golden oriole and the green woodpecker, are very easy to recognize. Some of the others are more difficult, but if you study the pictures you will soon learn the important features and be able to identify the birds when you spot them in the woods. Use a good guide book to help you with the many other birds you will see in the woods.

Bird Songs

Another way of identifying common birds in the woods is to learn their songs. You can buy or borrow recordings to help you, and then you will be able to impress your friends by telling them that there is a chiffchaff in the trees although you can't actually see it. The chiffchaff's song is actually an easy one to recognize: it sounds just like the bird's name repeated over and over again – *chiff-chaff-chiff-chaff-chiff-chaff*. This is, of course, how the bird got its name. Once you have heard the beautiful song of the nightingale on a recording you won't be able to mistake it in the woods. This drab brown bird sings by day as well as at night, but it is clearer at night when the other birds are quiet. Other easily recognized songs include those of the cuckoo and the woodpigeon. The latter has a rather soft five-note song with the second note long and loud and a distinct pause before the last two notes: *cu-cooo-coo——coo-coo*.

Male birds sing to defend their territories and to attract mates. Most birds also have other calls, shorter than their songs, which they use to call to their offspring or to warn of danger. The blackbird, for example, gives out a shrill *pink-pink-pink* when it is alarmed. Listen also for the rather strange drumming of the great spotted woodpecker as it hammers its beak on a dead branch like a pneumatic drill. This sound is used instead of a song to defend their territory and you will hear it mainly in the spring.

Bird Diets

Leaves are abundant in the woodlands, but very few birds actually eat leaves. The capercaillie of the northern coniferous forests is one of the few. It eats the shoots of pines and other conifers during the winter. Woodpigeons also eat lots of leaves, but these are usually stripped from the fields and not from the trees. Some finches, notably the bullfinch, feed on buds, but they don't eat mature leaves.

Fruits and seeds are much more important in the diets of woodland birds. Finches are essentially seed-eaters and they are equipped

Watching Birds

Birdwatcher

Jay

Binoculars are essential for every keen bird-watcher. They help you to pick out distinguishing marks and identify birds from a considerable distance. There are lots of different models, but if you are likely to do most of your birdwatching in the woods, where the light is often rather poor, you need a pair with good light-gathering power. This means a pair with fairly large objectives – the lenses furthest from your eyes. The larger these lenses, the more light they can pass to your eyes. But larger lenses are also heavy, so you must strike a balance. A pair marked 7 x 50 are good for night viewing and for woodland work. They magnify 7 times and the objectives are 50 mm across. Also fine for birdwatching are 8 x 30 and 8 x 40 binoculars, although the image might be a little dim in thick woodland. Be careful not to scratch the lenses on bushes and low branches.

WOODLAND BIRDS

Chiffchaff

Golden Oriole
(rare in Britain)

male

female

Great Spotted Woodpecker

female

male

Lesser
Spotted Woodpecker

male

female

Green Woodpecker

Coal Tit

Nuthatch

Treecreeper

male

female

male

female

Goldcrest

Woodpigeon

Crossbill

female

male

female

male

male
(winter)

Chaffinch

Nightingale

male

Redpoll

41

with stout beaks for crushing the seeds. The hawfinch's beak is so strong that it can crack open a cherry stone with ease. The crossbill is one of the most interesting finches. It uses the crossed tips of its beak to winkle out the seeds from the cones of pines and other conifers. The bird eats almost nothing else. Look for cones that it has attacked: the cone scales have been levered apart and broken, and those of spruce cones have usually been split right down the centre. Jays eat all kinds of food but are particularly fond of acorns. If you watch them in autumn you can see them flying from the oakwoods with their beaks and throats bulging with acorns, which they bury in surrounding areas as winter stores.

Insects are the main diet of many other woodland birds. Most of the insect-eaters have slender beaks. Watch the treecreeper running up tree trunks and probing the bark for insects. The nuthatch feeds in a similar way but can walk down the trunk as well. It also uses its powerful beak to open nuts, wedging them in bark crevices before hammering them apart. Look for the broken shells still jammed in the bark. Woodpeckers do much the same, but remove the empty shells and drop them on the ground below so that they can use the same crevice over and over again. As well as nuts, the woodpeckers eat large numbers of insects which they dig out from dead and dying trunks.

Nests Everywhere

Birds build their nests everywhere from ground level to the tree-tops, although each species has its prefered sites. Tits, for example, like to nest in tree holes. A dense shrub layer provides excellent cover for many warblers, which often nest very close to the ground. The nightjar actually nests on the ground. It makes no real nest but lays its eggs in a slight hollow. The sitting bird is almost invisible against the background of fallen leaves and twigs

It is against the law to disturb nesting birds, but when you are sure that they have left their nests for good you can examine the nests to see what they are made of.

Below: A female sparrowhawk guards her nest in a spruce tree. She and her mate are incredibly agile as they chase other birds through the trees. They must catch several small birds each day to feed themselves and their growing chicks.

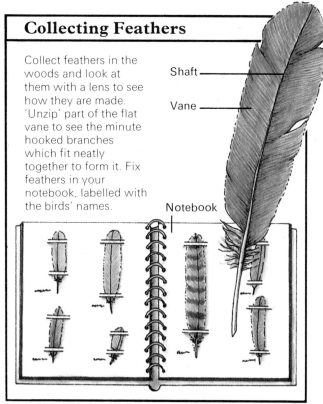

Collecting Feathers

Collect feathers in the woods and look at them with a lens to see how they are made. 'Unzip' part of the flat vane to see the minute hooked branches which fit neatly together to form it. Fix feathers in your notebook, labelled with the birds' names.

Shaft

Vane

Notebook

Woodland Mammals

Apart from the squirrels, most of our woodland mammals are active at night. Dusk and dawn are the best times to watch them in action, as long as you know where to look, but don't go to the woods alone. Deer are not difficult to find, especially the fallow deer. These live in fairly large herds and make conspicuous tracks through the woods. Look for their footprints in soft ground to show you where to go. They usually browse in clearings or along the edges of the woods, where you can watch them quite easily as long as you are careful about the wind direction. The wind must be blowing from the deer to you: if you approach from the wrong direction the animals will smell you and trot away before you get near enough to see them.

The flesh-eating mammals are more difficult to find and watch because most of them move about singly, but if you can find their homes and get in position before dusk you might see them come out. Badgers and foxes can be watched in this way. Badgers often romp about outside their burrows for a while, especially if they have cubs with them. A piece of red plastic fixed over your torch will enable you to observe these and other mammals because the animals' eyes are not very sensitive to the red light. Rarer mammals that you might be able to see in the woods are polecats, pine martens and wild cats. Lumps of meat or tinned pet food may attract them to your observation point, although none of these animals is really common. Look at their footprints after the animals have visited the bait. Stoats are often seen streaking across paths and clearings by day. Look for the black tip of the tail which distinguishes the stoat from its smaller cousin, the weasel.

Look out for other signs of animals: barbed wire around the woods is always worth examining for hairs left behind by mammals passing under or over the wire. The black and white hairs of the badger are easily identified, and so are the coarse hairs of deer. Other mammalian hairs can be identified, but only under a microscope. Piles of droppings will also give you clues about where to watch for the woodland mammals.

Right: The red squirrel is generally brick-red in summer, but greyer in winter, when it can be distinguished from the grey squirrel (above) by its ear tufts. Chewed cones and empty nut shells, often on tree stumps, show you where the squirrels have been eating.

Mammal Tracks

Mammal Tracks

A fox looks out from its den or earth. Foxes come out mainly at night. Look for their footprints (below) on muddy paths. They are similar to dog footprints but the two middle toes point inwards and they are much closer together. The surest sign of the fox, however, is its very strong smell.

A woodmouse explores a tree stump at night in search of food. The beech nuts in the picture will do very well. Notice the mouse's very large ears and eyes – both very necessary for finding its way and detecting danger at night. The animal also has a good sense of smell and uses its long whiskers to feel its way in the dark.

The common dormouse rarely ventures out by day. It feeds mainly in the bushes by night. It likes all kinds of fruits and seeds and here it is gnawing an unripe hazel nut – one of its favourite foods. Notice how the animal wraps its tail around a branch and uses it like an extra leg to cling firmly to the trees.

Making Plaster Casts

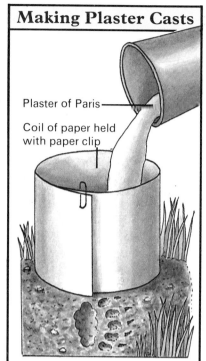

Plaster of Paris

Coil of paper held with paper clip

Badger print in the mud

Find a good clear footprint in the mud and surround it with a strip of thin card as shown above. Push the card well into the mud without disturbing the print. Mix some plaster of Paris in an old basin or large yoghurt pot and pour it into the circle of card. Leave it to set – about 20 minutes is usually long enough – and then dig it up. After washing, you will have a good cast of the animal's foot. You may need a little practice to get the mixture just right.

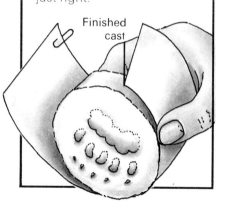

Finished cast

Badgers and Roe Deer

Watching Badgers

Big holes in woodland banks surrounded by lots of bare ground and scratched trees show you where badgers live, but you must go back at night to see the animals. Never go alone. Be in position, downwind of the holes, well before dusk and keep very quiet.

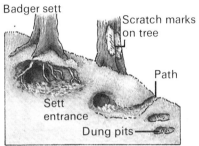

Badger sett

Scratch marks on tree

Path

Sett entrance

Dung pits

The Timid Roe Deer

The roe deer is the smallest of our native deer and, unlike most others, it does not live in herds. You will normally see just one at a time, or perhaps a small family group. Look for their footprints (below) in muddy paths. The animals are very shy and mainly nocturnal. You usually see them by accident, running rapidly away when you have disturbed their daytime rest. The animals are greyer in winter and then you can see the conspicuous white rump as they run. The males have antlers from late spring to late autumn and the antlers never have more than three points.

Roe deer footprint about one third natural size

Woodland Seasons

Spring

Bluebells carpet many beechwoods in the spring. Their leaves appear as winter turns to spring and the flowers follow in May, just as the beech leaves are beginning to open and cut off the light. The bluebell leaves continue to grow for another month or so, and then die away after pumping all their food into the bulbs ready for the next year. The best stands of flowers are to be found in the slightly more open areas where the leaves get more light and can make more food. Close to the beech trunks, where conditions are very shady and very dry in summer, there may be a few spindly bluebell plants, but they rarely flower in such places.

Summer

Throughout the summer the beech leaves are spread out so that they get the maximum amount of light to make food for the trees. Very little light reaches the ground. There are bright patches here and there, but they receive light only for short periods, when the sun can get through small chinks in the canopy, and few plants can grow there. Only in larger clearings, where a tree has fallen, can bracken and other plants thrive in the summer. Notice how the last autumn's leaves still carpet the ground. Their toughness, combined with the dryness of the woodland floor, means that they decay very slowly, so there are always plenty of dead leaves for you to shuffle through as you walk.

Woodland Seasons

Autumn

Autumn is a beautiful time in the beechwoods, with the leaves taking on their wonderful golden and coppery colours. Food is being rapidly withdrawn from the leaves at this time and stored in the twigs and branches ready for the following spring. Thin corky layers develop between the twigs and the leaf stalks and gradually cut off all water supplies to the leaves. The autumn winds then gradually blow the leaves from the trees. Some light then reaches the ground, but much more important is the rain reaching the ground. Decay of the previous year's leaves speeds up and crops of toadstools spring up on the woodland floor.

Winter

Even in winter there is quite a lot of shade in the beechwood. Look up at the branches and see how the twigs form a dense lattice. Look closely at one of the lower branches to see the narrow pointed buds so characteristic of the beech. At the base of the trunk you can see how the shallow roots spread out in all directions, sucking up all the available moisture and making the soil very dry. A few mosses grow here and there, especially on banks where they are above the carpet of dead leaves. Notice how smooth the beech bark is – another characteristic feature of this tree. It is often stained green by algae, especially on the shadier (northern) side of the trunk.

Tracks and Signs

Be a Wildlife Detective

Detectives search the scene of a crime for clues that might tell them who commited the crime. You too can be a wildlife detective, not trying to solve a crime but looking for clues to tell you what animals roam through the woods and other areas. Most birds and mammals leave their 'signatures' behind, and if you can read those signs you will be able to see where the animals have been and what they have been up to. Keep your eyes open and you will discover all kinds of clues with which to surprise your friends.

Footprints and Food Remains

Footprints are the commonest clues, especially in soft ground. The edges of ponds and puddles are good places to look, since many animals come to drink here and leave their tracks in the muddy ground.

Food remains can also tell you what animals live in your area. Hazel nuts split neatly in half are the work of squirrels, while nuts with neat round holes have been opened by mice or voles. Squirrels and mice also strip the scales from pine cones to get at the seeds, but mice make a neater job of it. Squirrels feed in the open and you will often find their left-overs on tree stumps in the woods.

Mice prefer to eat in private and you should look for their piles of nibbled nuts and cones under fallen branches and in the crevices around the base of the trees.

Clues in the Trees

Look for signs of damage to bark, for many mammals like to strip off pieces of bark to get at the soft tissues just underneath it. This is especially true in the winter when there are fewer leaves to eat. Deer dig their lower teeth into the bark and pull, leaving jagged edges at the top of the wound. Another good sign of deer, assuming there are no cattle or horses around, is the trimming of the lower branches at a fixed height. This is especially marked around the edges of the woodland and it shows the maximum height that the deer can reach to nibble the leaves and twigs.

Even insects leave clues in the form of chewed leaves and scattered black droppings on the lower vegetation. This is a good way of finding caterpillars, which are often very well camouflaged and difficult to spot. Keep your eyes open for moths resting on the tree trunks. When you get your eye in you will be surprised at how many camouflaged moths you can find.

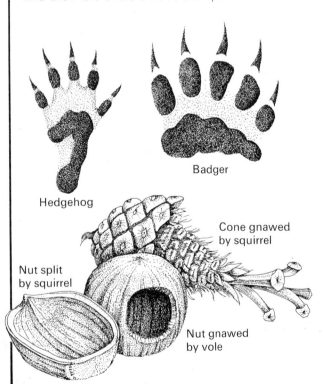

Hedgehog

Badger

Nut split by squirrel

Cone gnawed by squirrel

Nut gnawed by vole

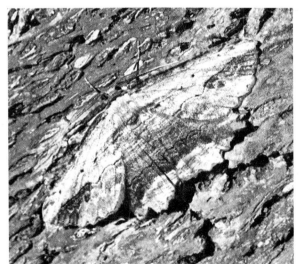

Left: Footprints and food remains are the commonest signs to look for. Droppings also show you where to look for animals.

Above: The waved umber moth lines itself up with the bark crevices on tree trunks. You will need sharp eyes to spot it.

FIELDS AND HEDGEROWS

The European grasslands are nearly all artificial habitats, which have been created by people and their grazing animals over the last few thousand years. Left to themselves, without any sheep or rabbits to nibble the plants, the grasslands would gradually turn back into woodland once more. Some hedgerows are the remains of ancient woodlands but many were planted by people to form boundaries to their fields.

Explore the fields and hedgerows in your area and discover the secret life of the grasses and other flowering plants in this fascinating habitat. Find out how to tell the age of a hedge and how to recognize some of the common birds and butterflies of the fields and hedgerows. Learn how to tell the difference between a mole and a vole or a rabbit and a hare.

A Grassland Walk

Dropping down from the brow of the hill, the footpath passes through rough grassland. A couple of rabbits scuttle away as you approach, and a grass snake slithers noiselessly out of sight. It will be back to continue sunbathing on the path when you have gone. The well-worn track is as hard as rock, but daisies and greater plantains manage to survive there. Their leaves lie flat on the ground and come to little harm if you tread on them, but the flowers are short and stunted. A song thrush has chosen a flat stone on the path as an anvil on which to break snail shells. Look at the broken shells around the stone. If you keep quiet the thrush may return to hammer another one open: she may even bring her young so that they can learn how to break the shells and get at the soft snails inside.

The surrounding grassland, grazed by only a few rabbits, has grown quite tall. It is dotted with wild flowers which attract meadow brown and common blue butterflies. Watch how their hair-like tongues probe the flowers to reach the sweet nectar. In the shadow of the hedge the hogweed spreads its flower-heads like a group of lace-covered tables, and many insects come to lap up the nectar. Purple knapweed mingles with the hogweed, but a marbled white butterfly has no trouble in finding its nectar-filled flowers.

As you approach the stile a magnificent scene unfolds. Much of the land is cultivated, but in the distance you can see the rough grazings on the hillsides. Too steep for ploughing, these slopes have been grazed by sheep for centuries and this has prevented any trees from growing. Look at the brilliant red poppies bordering the wheat field close to the

51

A Grassland Walk

The Grasshopper's Song

Male grasshoppers, which you can recognize by the upturned tip of the abdomen, 'sing' to attract females. The 'song' is produced by rubbing the back legs against the wings. Tiny pegs on the inside of the legs make the sound as they pass over a hard vein on each wing. You can make similar sounds by drawing the teeth of a comb over your thumb nail. Each kind of grasshopper has its own 'song'.

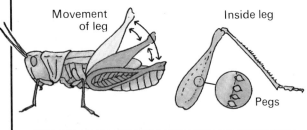

Movement of leg

Inside leg

Pegs

stile. The farmer sprays his crops to kill these weeds, but those on the margin often escape. More will come up the next year, and the next, for poppies scatter huge numbers of seeds which can survive in the soil for a long time, perhaps for as long as a hundred years. Every year the plough turns up another batch ready to grow.

Lower down, on the rich soils of the valley, you can see the haymaking in full swing in the meadows and the cattle grazing peacefully on the pastures. Few flowers grow in these fields because the farmer sows special grass seed mixtures to provide rich food for his cattle. Notice the hedges dividing the fields. Some are very old, for the land has been cultivated for many centuries. We need to grow food in the fields, but the wise farmer makes sure that hedges and other areas remain for wild plants and animals.

To explore and understand the wildlife of all the grassland habitats seen on this walk you will need very little equipment apart from your eyes and a notebook for recording observations and experiments. A hand lens (× 10 is a practical size) will be very useful for close examinations as well as binoculars (see page 19) for watching and identifying birds and other animals from a distance.

Growing Uninvited Guests

Lots of hooked fruits cling to your socks and other clothes during a country walk. Some common ones are shown here. Try growing some in a seed tray. The hooks are really designed to cling to animal fur, and by the time they fall off they are a long way from their original homes. This is how the plants spread to new areas. You can also carry seeds in the mud on your shoes. Scrape the mud into a seed tray and see how many plants grow from it.

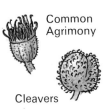

Common Agrimony

Cleavers

Burdock

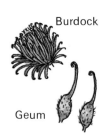

Geum

Grasses of the Field

Dozens of different kinds of grasses grow in the fields and on the open hillsides and roadside verges. They all look much alike until their flower-heads shoot up in June, and then you can usually pick out several different kinds even in a small area. Some of the commoner grasses are illustrated below. Notice how the flower-heads differ. Some form narrow spikes, others form clusters or graceful sprays. Each flower-head consists of a number of oval spikelets, and each spikelet is composed of papery scales enclosing one or more tiny flowers. The scales are green at first, but become brown or golden as the seeds ripen. The flowers have no petals and no scent or nectar. They rely on the wind to carry pollen from flower to flower for pollination. Until this happens no seeds can develop.

Most grass flowers have three stamens and two feathery stigmas. Look closely at the grasses when their flowers open and you will see the stamens hanging from the spikelets and swaying in the slightest breeze. Pollen is blown from them and some lands on the stigmas to trigger off the development of the seeds. Unfortunately for many people, breathing the grass pollen up their noses causes the unpleasant condition known as hay fever. The months of June and July are the worst for this, because this is when most of the grasses are in flower.

The whole flower-head and stalk dies when the seeds have been scattered, and in the annual grasses the whole plant dies, leaving just the seeds for the following year. Our cultivated cereals, which are simply grasses with large edible grains, are of this type. But most grasses are perennials and, although the old flower-heads die, plenty of leafy shoots remain at the base. Some of these will produce the next year's flower-heads.

Some grasses form thick tufts, while others produce a continuous turf. Grazing, as long as

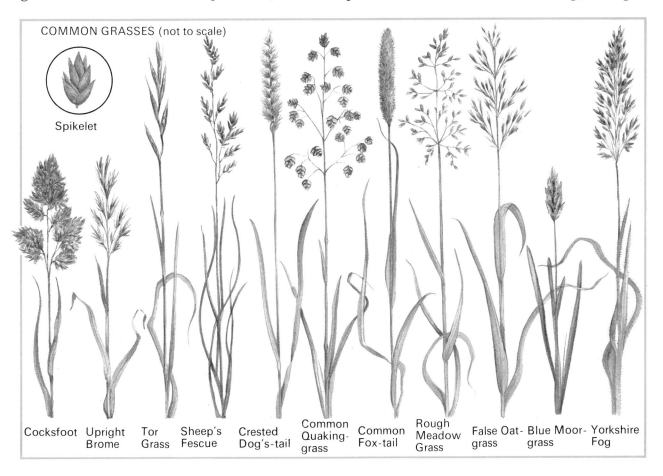

COMMON GRASSES (not to scale)

Spikelet

Cocksfoot   Upright Brome   Tor Grass   Sheep's Fescue   Crested Dog's-tail   Common Quaking-grass   Common Fox-tail   Rough Meadow Grass   False Oat-grass   Blue Moor-grass   Yorkshire Fog

Field Projects

Fields and Meadows

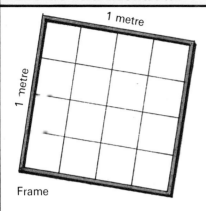

Frame

1 metre

1 metre

Toss it over your shoulder

The grassland community differs from place to place. Some plants like dry ground and some prefer damp areas, some like sandy soils and others like chalk. You can explore the differences between various fields by counting the numbers of each plant species in a square metre. Make a simple frame, 1-metre square, as shown in the picture. The strings, 25 centimetres apart, help with the counting, but are not essential. Throw the frame down at random several times in each field and list the plants you find in each square. A field guide will help you to identify them even when they are not in flower. Fields with more flowers than others are likely to be grazed less often.

Pressing Wild Flowers

Picking and pressing wild flowers for a collection is a good way of learning about the many different kinds of flowers. Learn to recognize them from the shapes of the petals and leaves and from the numbers of petals and stamens.

The easiest way to preserve the flowers is to press them under a pile of books. Arrange the flowers neatly between sheets of clean blotting paper, cover them with some sheets of newspaper, and then add some heavy books. Change the paper after a few days if it is damp. The plants should be dry after a couple of weeks and you can then transfer them to a loose-leaf notebook. Label each one carefully. Pick only the common flowers that you see around you.

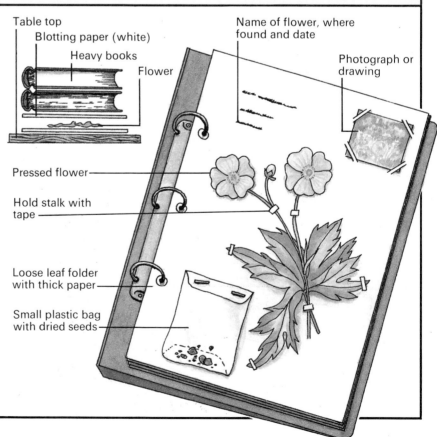

Table top
Blotting paper (white)
Heavy books
Flower

Name of flower, where found and date

Photograph or drawing

Pressed flower

Hold stalk with tape

Loose leaf folder with thick paper

Small plastic bag with dried seeds

it is not too severe, helps to form turf because it encourages new shoots to spread out at ground level. Mowing does the same. Notice how quickly the grass grows again after grazing or mowing. The leaves grow continuously from the base and soon make good the damage. If they could not do this, grasses could not survive regular grazing.

Grassland Flowers

The majority of our grasslands have been created by sheep grazing during the last few thousand years and are not truly natural. They nevertheless support huge numbers of wild flowers, especially on the unploughed hillsides and commons. You will be surprised at the number of different kinds of flowers that you can find if you really look. Use a good guide book to help you to name them. Explore as many different kinds of grassland as you can and see which kinds of flowers grow in each place.

Examine footpaths and other heavily trampled areas of grassland. You will find fewer kinds of plants here than in the untrodden areas because not many can withstand the constant passage of feet. Among those that can survive on the paths are the dandelion, the greater plantain and the little daisy. Their leaf rosettes lie flat on the ground and are not damaged when you tread on them. If you have plantains on your lawn, try digging a couple up and replanting them in a shady corner of the garden. You will find that they produce much larger, upright leaves, showing that it is the exposure to full light that keeps them flat in trampled areas.

The greatest variety of wild flowers is to be found in lightly grazed areas and also in some ancient hay meadows. Where there is no grazing at all the taller grasses quickly swamp the shorter flowers and, as we shall see later, bushes and trees soon invade the grassland. Heavy grazing, just like regular trampling,

Protected Flowers

Never dig up wild flowers for your garden or for any other reason. This spoils the countryside for other people and is against the law in Britain. Many of our wild flowers have become rare because thoughtless people dug them up in the past. Some of our rarest species must not even be picked: they can't set seeds if you pick them. Never pick unusual flowers – only the ones you know are common.

Right: This picture taken from ground level reveals the wealth of plant life there is in a meadow. Tall grasses tower above the grassland 'jungle', with bird's-foot trefoil and field mouse-ear growing beneath them. Explore the grassland at ground level yourself.

Grassland Flowers

also destroys most of the flowers. If the grazing is particularly severe – around rabbit warrens, for example – even the grass may be destroyed.

In the lightly grazed areas many of the flowers spring from low-growing mats or rosettes of leaves. These ground-hugging leaves get plenty of light because the grasses around them are regularly nibbled and kept quite short, but the mats and rosettes themselves are rarely eaten. Good examples of these low-growing plants include the wild thyme, cowslip and rockrose – all of which are pictured on the right. Low growth is particularly useful on the drier grasslands, for the leaves then escape the worst of the wind and do not lose as much water. Many of the plants growing on the chalk hills, which are well-drained and often very dry in the summer, have extremely long roots. The roots of the salad burnet, for example, may plunge down more than 60 centimetres. They will always find water at such depths.

Shiny yellow buttercups dot the fields and hillsides from early spring until the autumn. Look carefully at the flowers and you will see that there are two common species. The meadow buttercup likes rich and slightly damp soil. It has smooth flower stalks and its sepals cradle the petals when the flowers open. The bulbous buttercup prefers drier grasslands, especially on lime-rich soils. Its flower stalks are grooved and its sepals turn down when the flowers are open. The bulbous buttercup has usually finished flowering by the end of June.

The Curious Orchids

Many orchids grow in the grasslands of Europe. They are not as showy as their tropical cousins, but their flowers are still fascinating. The bee orchid, which you can

Right: These flowers can all be found in fields, meadows and roadside verges. The rockrose, meadow clary and bee orchid grow only on lime-rich soils. The snake's-head fritillary is very rare: never pick it if you are lucky enough to find one. Look for it in old damp meadows.

GRASSLAND FLOWERS

Bulbous Buttercup

Salad Burnet   Meadow Cranesbill   Meadow Buttercup

Meadow Vetchling   Sainfoin   Bird's-foot Trefoil

Field Scabious   Knapweed   Common Rockrose

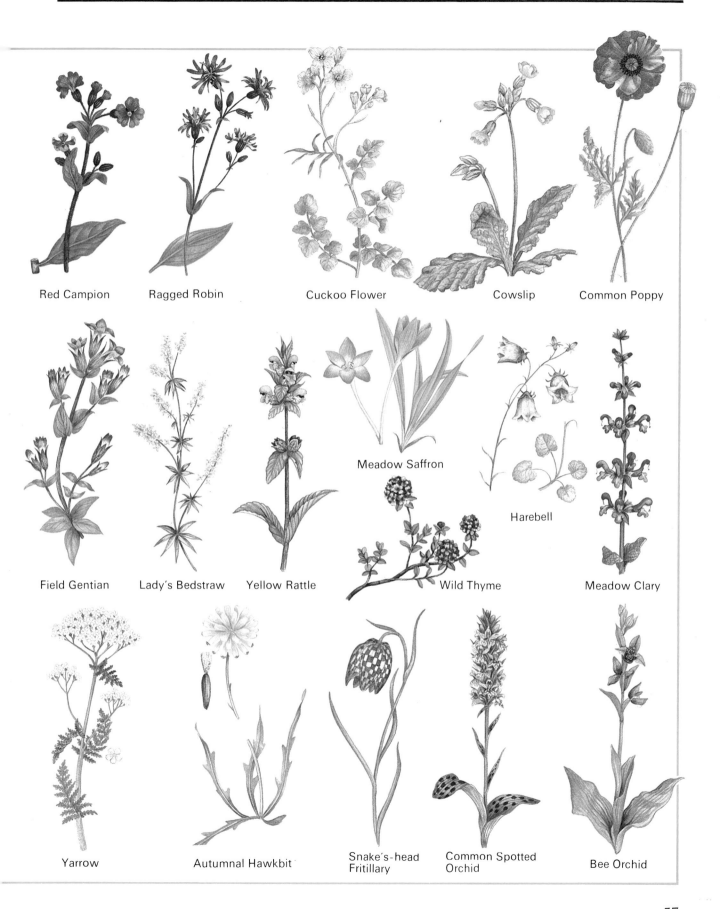

Red Campion

Ragged Robin

Cuckoo Flower

Cowslip

Common Poppy

Field Gentian

Lady's Bedstraw

Yellow Rattle

Meadow Saffron

Harebell

Wild Thyme

Meadow Clary

Yarrow

Autumnal Hawkbit

Snake's-head Fritillary

Common Spotted Orchid

Bee Orchid

57

Grassland Insects

see on page 57, has a flower that looks just like a bee. The man orchid has a yellowish flower resembling a tiny man hanging from the stalk, while the lady orchid flower is shaped just like a woman wearing a wide skirt.

Insects of the Grassland

Huge numbers of insects live amongst the grasses and other plants of the fields. Use nets like the ones shown below to catch some of the insects: you will be amazed at how many different kinds occur in just a small area. Get down on your knees and examine the ground around the bottoms of the grasses. Lots of small insects live here, feeding on dead and decaying leaves and other rubbish. Many also rest here during the day and crawl up the plants to feed at night.

If you walk through any rough grassland in the summer you will hear the grasshoppers chirping to each other. Turn back to page 4 to find out how they make their buzzing sounds. Some of them whirr just like miniature sewing machines. The grasshoppers fly up when you walk through the grass, but soon settle again and are very difficult to spot because their green and brown bodies blend so well with the grasses. This camouflage protects the grasshoppers from birds and lizards, which are their main enemies. Some continental grasshoppers have bright red or blue hind wings which show up clearly in flight. When the insects drop to the ground again they cover the hind wings with their drab brown front wings and become very hard to find. Birds which have been following

Using a Sweep Net

Grasshoppers, caterpillars and other insects living in the grass can be collected with a sturdy net called a sweep net. Don't use an ordinary butterfly net for this because it would soon get damaged. Sweep the net from side to side through the vegetation in front of you. Examine it after every two or three sweeps to see what you have caught. You will find lots of spiders and small flies in the net. Use your lens to have a close look before releasing them.

Using a Butterfly Net

A butterfly net can be used to catch all sorts of flying insects. You can buy one or make one. The frame should be at least 30 centimetres across and the bag should be about 60 centimetres deep so that you can fold it over to trap the insects that you catch. Make the bag from fine netting. Black and dark green are the best colours. Be careful not to snag the net on brambles. It is often easier to catch a butterfly on the wing than one sitting on flowers.

Grassland Insects

Breeding Caterpillars

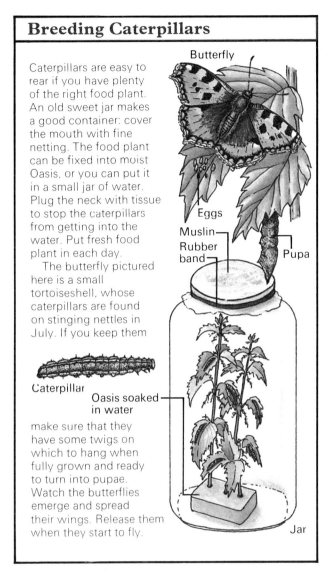

Caterpillars are easy to rear if you have plenty of the right food plant. An old sweet jar makes a good container: cover the mouth with fine netting. The food plant can be fixed into moist Oasis, or you can put it in a small jar of water. Plug the neck with tissue to stop the caterpillars from getting into the water. Put fresh food plant in each day.

The butterfly pictured here is a small tortoiseshell, whose caterpillars are found on stinging nettles in July. If you keep them

make sure that they have some twigs on which to hang when fully grown and ready to turn into pupae. Watch the butterflies emerge and spread their wings. Release them when they start to fly.

the bright colours are totally confused. Many people are also puzzled, thinking they have seen brightly coloured butterflies disappear without trace.

Walking through the grasslands in late spring or early summer, watch out for blobs of white froth on the plants. Often there are so many that you get your legs wet. Generally known as cuckoo-spit, the froth has nothing in fact to do with cuckoos. Look inside one of the blobs and you will find a small green insect. It is a young froghopper, which feeds by sucking sap from the plant through its needle-like beak. It surrounds itself with the froth to shield it from the dry air. The froth also gives some protection against birds, but

The Meadow Brown Butterfly

The meadow brown is one of our commonest butterflies. You can see it flitting rather lazily over all kinds of grassland in the summer. The one in the picture is feeding at a thistle. Notice its slender tongue probing the flower for nectar. Notice also the eye-spot near the wing-tip. Birds peck at this instead of the real eye: the wing is damaged but the insect is not really hurt.

some enemies know that a juicy insect can be found under the bubbles. Adult froghoppers are small brown jumping insects, not unlike miniature frogs. You will find lots in your sweep net. They suck sap but do not live under froth. You will also find some black and red froghoppers whose bold pattern warns birds that they are not nice to eat. Bold patterns and bright colours like this are known as warning colours.

Grassland Butterflies

Flowery hillsides and roadside verges teem with butterflies in the summer. The insects are attracted by the sweet nectar of knapweeds, thistles, and many other flowers. Some well-known grassland butterflies are illustrated on page 13. The meadow brown (above) is one of the commonest species. It belongs to the family known as the browns. All members of the family have eye-spots around the edges of their wings. The

59

Butterflies and Moths

gatekeeper or hedge brown is very common along hedgerows and the edges of woods in southern Britain. Despite its colour, the marbled white also belongs to the brown family: look for its eye-spots. It is especially fond of knapweed and scabious flowers. All the caterpillars in this family feed on grasses.

The swallowtail is extremely rare in Britain, and is only found in a small area of the Norfolk Broads. On the continent, however, many can be seen on dry grassland as well as in damper areas. The scarce swallowtail is actually common on rough grassland in southern Europe.

Several kinds of blue butterfly can be found in grassland. The females are often brown, sometimes with just a few blue scales close to the body. The caterpillars of this group often feed on clovers and vetches. The skippers are fast-flying little butterflies that dart from flower to flower so quickly that you often lose sight of them. They often sit on the flowers with their wings half open.

Moths of Grasslands

Moths are even more common than butterflies, but most of them fly at night and you normally see them only if you disturb them as you walk. The brightly coloured burnet moths fly by day, however, and are often thought to be butterflies. Look for them on the flowers of scabious and knapweed. You can often pick them up, as they are rather sleepy insects. Their bright red spots warn birds that they have a very nasty taste, and the birds soon learn to avoid them. Examine the grass stalks in June for their papery yellow cocoons: you might see the burnet moths emerging from them.

The cinnabar moth is another black and red moth with a nasty taste, although this moth generally flies by night. Watch out for its

Right: The silken tents of the caterpillar of the small ermine moth are common on hedgerows in spring. Notice how the caterpillars have eaten all the leaves in the tent. The adult moth is a delicate insect with black dots all over its white wings. Several other kinds of caterpillars make tent webs.

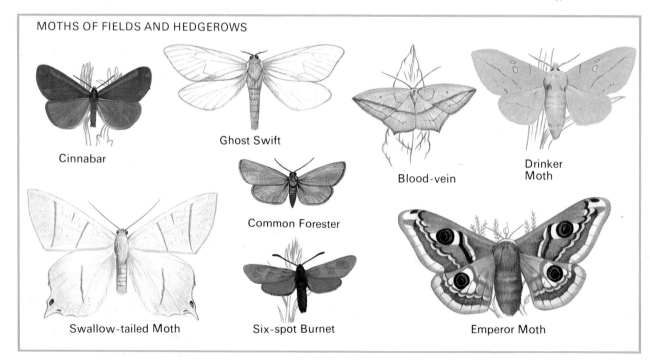

MOTHS OF FIELDS AND HEDGEROWS

Cinnabar

Ghost Swift

Blood-vein

Drinker Moth

Swallow-tailed Moth

Common Forester

Six-spot Burnet

Emperor Moth

Identifying Butterflies

GRASSLAND BUTTERFLIES

Dark Green Fritillary

female

Gatekeeper

male

male

caterpillar

Marbled White

caterpillar

male

female

male

Dingy Skipper

female

male

male

Small Heath

Clouded Yellow

female

Common Blue

Orange Tip

caterpillar

caterpillar

female

male

male

Small Copper

Swallowtail
(very rare in Britain)

Large Skipper

Chalk Hill Blue

Great Banded Grayling
(not found in Britain)

Scarce Swallowtail
(not found in Britain)

Grizzled Skipper

Beetles

black and gold caterpillars on ragwort plants in July. The caterpillars also taste bad and birds avoid them.

Male emperor moths fly in the sunshine, generally in the afternoon, and can be seen skimming very fast over scrubby grassland and along hedgerows in April and May. They are using their huge feathery antennae to sniff out the plumper and greyer females. The latter do not fly until nightfall, when they lay their eggs on various kinds of plants.

The ghost moth flies at dusk in the summer and gets its name because of the male's eerie flight. The male is pure white on the upper side and dark brown below. As it dances up and down, you see only flashes of white. The yellowish female is attracted to the 'dance' and the insects then mate.

Beetles of all Sizes

Your sweep net will capture large numbers of beetles as you work your way through the grasses and other plants. Many of these beetles will be very small but you can easily recognize them by their hard wing cases covering most of the body. These wing cases are often very shiny, but if you look at them through a hand lens you will see that some are coated with minute scales. Many of the beetles belong to the group known as weevils. You can recognize these by the long snout.

Look for larger beetles crawling on the ground. The bloody-nosed beetle is a rather round black beetle that gives out a drop of bright red blood from its mouth when you squeeze it. This habit is thought to frighten birds that peck at it. If there are rabbits in the area you might well find the shiny black minotaur beetle. This is one of the dung beetles and it buries rabbit droppings as food for both adult and young. The male has a long horn on each side of the thorax (the middle of the three main body sections) and a shorter one in the centre.

Watch for glow-worms on summer evenings just as it is getting dark. The female sits on the grass and gives out a greenish light from her hind end. She may put her light out if you pick her up, but she often goes on glowing. She has no wings and looks rather like a brown woodlouse, but she is actually a beetle. The male has wings and looks much more like a beetle, although his wing covers are quite soft. He flies over the grassland and is attracted to the female's light. Young glow-worms feed on snails.

Grassland Refuse Disposal

The brightly coloured beetle in this picture is a burying beetle or sexton beetle, one of nature's huge army of scavengers which get rid of dung and the bodies of dead animals. Burying beetles work in pairs in the breeding season and quickly bury the bodies of small animals like the shrew seen here. They do this by digging the soil from below the corpses. They then feed on the flesh, and also lay their eggs on or near the flesh so that their grubs have plenty to eat.

Grassland Snails and Reptiles

In some southern parts of Europe you might be lucky enough to see the glow-worm's cousin the firefly. Both the male and the female have wings, although the female does not fly, and both produce light. The males fly low over the ground and produce short flashes of light every second. The females sit in the grass and reply with their own flashes. The males then come down and the beetles mate.

Grassland Snails

Snails need plenty of lime to make their shells and are most common in chalky areas and on other lime-rich soils. Most of them feed on dead and rotting leaves. The brown-lipped snail is one of the commonest. Its shell is usually yellow or pink, with up to five brown bands on each whorl. The lip is brown. The white-lipped snail is very similar except for its white lip. Both are commonly called banded snails. The shell of the striped snail is also rather similar, although its shell is basically white. If you turn it upside down you will see a narrow hole called the umbilicus. In the banded snails this hole is completely covered by the lip. The striped snail often clusters on plants in dry weather.

Keep a special watch for the round-mouthed snail on chalk and limestone. It is one of the few land snails that close their shells with a horny disc like that of the winkle.

Snakes and Lizards

The snakes and lizards belong to the large group of animals called reptiles. They are generally described as cold-blooded animals, but their bodies actually stay at the same

Above: Examine grassland snail shells for glow-worm grubs. Here is one eating into a snail.

Below: If you find a snake watch how it picks up scent by flicking its tongue out. This is a grass snake.

A Thrush's Anvil

Thrush

Broken shells

Anvil

Look for the song thrush's anvil – a large stone, often at the side of a path, on which the bird hammers open snail shells. Examine the broken shells. Most of them belong to the banded snails and are yellowish with up to five brown bands. Some have no bands at all. Work out which shells are the best camouflaged on rough grassland. Which shells are most often collected by the thrush? Try to find living snails in the grass yourself.

Snakes and Lizards

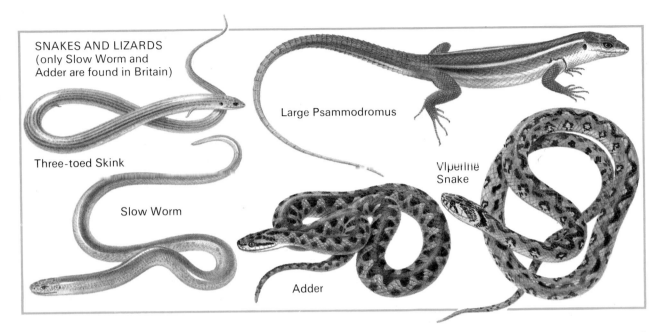

SNAKES AND LIZARDS
(only Slow Worm and
Adder are found in Britain)

Three-toed Skink

Slow Worm

Large Psammodromus

Viperine Snake

Adder

temperature as the surroundings and are sometimes quite hot. They are very sluggish in cold weather, and they sleep right through the winter in Europe. Only three kinds of snakes and three kinds of lizards live in Britain, but there are many more in the warmer parts of Europe. Most like to sunbathe in the mornings to warm up, and this is a good time to look for them. As they get warm, they get much more active and more difficult to find – you may see only a tail disappearing into the grass. All the reptiles have scaly skins and they are not at all slimy.

Snakes have no legs, but they glide very efficiently over the ground. They like to coil around clumps of grass or the base of bushes for sunbathing. Walk quietly if you want to see them, for they can pick up the vibrations of your footsteps and may be frightened away. The adder is the only poisonous snake in Britain. You can recognize it by the dark zig-zag pattern on its back. It lives on both dry and damp grassland and feeds on lizards and small mammals. The grass snake prefers damp grassland and is common around ponds and streams. It swims well and frogs are its favourite prey. Look for the yellowish collar to identify this snake.

Lizards are generally very agile and difficult to catch, but make good pets if you have a suitable cage such as an old fish tank. They like rough grassland with rocky areas or bare ground for sunbathing. Many live on and around walls in the southern parts of Europe and are known as wall lizards. Watch them dart after insects, which are the main foods of most lizards. The viviparous lizard is the commonest British species. Its eggs hatch

Sun-loving Lizards

This wall lizard is living up to its name and enjoying a spot of sunbathing on an old wall. If you approach very carefully, with no sudden movement, you can get quite close to basking lizards. Be careful not to let your shadow fall on them or they will dart away in a flash and may not reappear for a long time.

more or less as they are being laid. Look for the pregnant females basking in the sun to speed up the development of their eggs. The slow worm is a legless lizard with a liking for lush grassland. It feeds mainly on slugs. Look for it after rain, or else search under flat stones and old planks or sheets of corrugated iron. Don't mistake it for the three-toed skink of southern Europe which looks like a slow worm but has tiny legs.

In southern Europe, keep an eye open for large green lizards. As well as eating insects they sometimes take baby birds and mammals and even gobble up other lizards. Do not be surprised to find lizards without tails. If a lizard is caught by the tail, it can snap it off and escape – leaving the bird or other enemy holding just the wriggling tail. The lizard grows a new tail later.

Birds of the Fields

Walk over farmland or grassy hillsides at any time of the year and you will almost certainly catch a glimpse of the skylark. This is truly a bird of the open spaces, keeping well away from trees and hedgerows and spending all of its time either on the ground or in the air. It feeds on seeds and insects and you can watch it quite easily as it roams over farmland in winter. Your binoculars will pick out the small crest on the head and the white edges to the tail. In spring and summer you are more likely to see the skylark high in the air, although you will probably hear it long before you see it. The males rise almost vertically to heights up to 300 metres and hover there for long periods while pouring out their shrill, warbling song. They usually sing directly above their nests, which are always built on the ground. Do not try to find the nests: they are very well camouflaged and you could easily tread on them without seeing them.

The meadow pipit is another rather drab brown, ground-nesting bird and you might easily mistake it for the skylark. It has no crest, however, and its beak is thinner than that of the skylark. Like the skylark, its drab

Below: The graceful hen harrier swoops over the wilder grasslands. This is a female: the male is grey.

Birds of the Fields

colour camouflages it against predators. The meadow pipit produces its high-pitched trilling song while rising to a height of about 30 metres and then gliding down again. It does not hover. Meadow pipits like most kinds of open country but, unlike the skylark, they do not nest on cultivated land.

The pictures below show some of the many small birds that breed and feed in the grasslands. Several of them nest on the ground but, apart from the skylark, meadow pipit and wheatear, they like to stay close to hedgerows or scattered shrubs. Listen for the song of the yellowhammer, consisting of a series of very short notes followed by a long one. The song is commonly translated as '*a little bit of bread and no chee-ee-ee-se*'.

The birds shown opposite are all larger species than the ones below. Rooks and carrion crows both nest in trees but com-

GRASSLAND BIRDS

female

male

Yellowhammer

male female

Linnet

male

female

Wheatear

Meadow Pipit

Long-tailed tit

male

female

Whitethroat

Redwing

Fieldfare

female male

Stonechat

Skylark

monly feed on farmland. They take some seed from ploughed land, but also devour many harmful insects, such as cockchafer grubs, and snap up insects on cow-pats. Dead animals are also eaten – you often see the birds pecking at rabbits that have been killed on the road. To learn how to spot the difference between a rook and a crow look at their beaks and legs. The hooded crow is really just a form of the carrion crow.

Binoculars for Bird-watching

There are many sizes and models of binoculars on the market. Don't be tempted to go for the biggest and most powerful: these will be very heavy to carry. A pair marked 8×40 giving you a magnification of 8, is ideal for normal bird-watching. If you can afford a lightweight pair, choose one marked 10×24 or thereabouts.

light-breasted form

dark-breasted form

Barn Owl

female

male

Kestrel

Curlew

Carrion Crow

Rook

Hooded Crow

Short-eared Owl

male

female

Lapwing

Partridge

male

female

Pheasant

Birds of Prey

Lapwings, also known as peewits from the sound of their calls, are common on farmland after harvest. Watch them moving across the fields in large flocks as they search for seeds and insects. They often take flight together and perform spectacular aerial displays. You can see the birds on pastures and rough grasslands throughout the year. They nest on the ground where the grasses are not too tall.

Birds of Prey

The open grasslands are superb hunting grounds for many birds of prey. The best known of these hunters is the kestrel, also called the windhover because of the wonderful way in which it hovers almost motionless on the air. Look for it over roadside and motorway verges as well as fields and hillsides, and notice how the tail feathers fan out to give the bird extra lift. Although it might hover as much as 30 metres above the ground, its sharp eyes spot any movement on the ground. Watch how the kestrel plunges down to investigate: you might even see it rise again with a vole securely gripped in its talons. Field voles (see page 70) are the kestrel's main prey and a fully grown bird will usually eat the equivalent of two voles each day. Other foods include mice and shrews, beetles, grasshoppers and small birds.

The hen harrier is a spectacular bird of prey which usually operates over wilder grasslands. Swooping low over the grass, and banking and turning majestically at the end of each run, the bird gradually covers a wide area in its search for food. Small birds and mammals, including rabbits, are the harrier's main prey. Long wings enable the harrier to make quick, elegant turns when it spots one of these and its long legs are lowered to snatch the animal from the ground.

The short-eared owl hunts in much the same way as the harrier and, unlike most other owls, it flies in the daytime. By night, its place is taken by the barn owl, whose white underside gives it a very ghostly appearance as it glides swiftly over the fields. The barn owl can screech and hiss loudly but it is silent when hunting and this makes its flight even more ghostlike.

Observing Rabbits

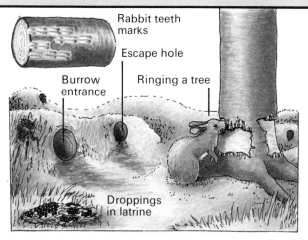

Rabbit teeth marks

Escape hole

Ringing a tree

Burrow entrance

Droppings in latrine

Rabbits are best seen in the evening or early in the morning, but it is very easy to find out where they live. Look for their burrows, surrounded by lots of bare soil where the animals have chewed away all the turf. As in the photograph above there may be plenty of ragwort instead, which the rabbits don't like and won't eat. Look for other tell-tale signs, such as piles of droppings – often placed on ant hills – and gnawed bark around the bases of trees. The rabbit's two front teeth are grooved in the front edge and when the animals chew bark they leave a narrow strip in the centre of each tooth mark. These animals eat bark mainly during the winter months.

Grassland Mammals

As we have already seen, the grasses are the only plants able to stand up to regular grazing. In areas of natural grassland we find large herds of grazing mammals – bison on the American prairies, antelopes on the African savannas and kangaroos on the Australian grasslands. Apart from some mountain pastures, European grasslands are not natural and so we have no such grazing herds. The largest of our truly wild grazers, other than goats and other mountain animals, are the hares and rabbits.

Look for the brown hare in pastures and rough grassland and also on cultivated land. It is quite easy to spot in grain fields in the spring, before the cereals grow too high. You might even see the hare's famous spring 'boxing matches', in which two or more males chase each other and often stand on their hind legs to fight. This behaviour gave rise to the expression 'mad as a March hare'. Dawn and dusk are the best times for watching hares, but they are often active in the middle of the day in areas where they are not disturbed. The brown hare's ears are much larger than those of a rabbit, and when the animal moves you will see that its legs are also much longer. Whereas the rabbit scuttles along on its short legs, the hare goes in leaps and bounds.

Hares do not make burrows. They sleep on the surface on a flattened area of grass called a form. With their ears pulled down along the back, it is surprising how easily they can hide amongst the grasses. The young, called leverets, are born in a form and, unlike baby rabbits, they are fully furred and have their eyes open.

Mischievous Rabbits

The rabbit was once confined to Spain and Portugal, but has now spread to nearly all parts of Europe. The Normans brought it to Britain in the 12th century. Rabbits can destroy many field crops and young tree plantations and are a serious pest in many areas. The hare can also be a pest, but is generally a solitary animal and does less harm than the rabbits which live in colonies. Each colony inhabits a collection of burrows known as a warren. This is always close to some kind of shelter, in the form of rocks or hedgerows, and never right out in the open. Many rabbits live in the woodland if there are surrounding fields for them to feed in. They are mainly nocturnal but, like the hare, they come out by day in undisturbed areas. Constant nibbling keeps the grass very short around the warren. The ground may be quite bare close to the entrances, but ragwort and stinging nettles may grow here because the rabbits will not eat these plants.

You must keep very still and very quiet if you want to watch rabbits. It is best to use binoculars from a distance. If any rabbits see you they will warn the others by thumping the ground with their hind legs. The bobbing white tails of the scurrying rabbits also warn others of danger. Look for skulls and other bones around the warren. Notice that there

Signs of the Brown Hare

Form

A flattened patch of grass may indicate a hare's form – an area where it rests and even gives birth to its babies called leverets. When resting in its form, the hare lays its long ears back along its body and it is then very hard to see even in fairly short grass. It keeps very still if it senses danger.

Small Mammals

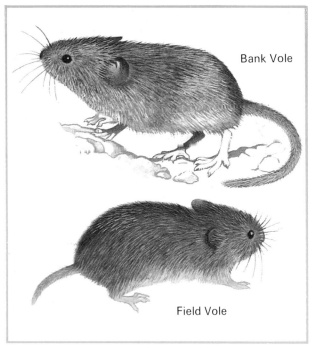

Bank Vole

Field Vole

The Hidden World of the Mole

Mound   Running tunnel   Mound

Chamber

Moles make complex tunnel systems in the soil. The excavated soil is pushed up to form mole hills. Sleeping and nesting chambers are dug out here and there, and extra large mole hills develop above these. Some chambers are also used for storing worms. The mole may also tunnel just beneath the surface, pushing up a ridge instead of scattered mole hills.

are two very tiny teeth just behind the big front teeth in the upper jaw. Only rabbits and hares have these extra teeth.

Although rabbits do a lot of damage to crops and young trees, they do help to keep our grasslands open. When most of the rabbits died in the 1950s from a disease called myxomatosis, the open hillsides were quickly taken over by bushes and shrubs: some have now been converted to woodland.

Voles and Moles

The field vole is the commonest grassland mammal in Britain although it cannot survive in heavily grazed areas. Look for its runways criss-crossing the ground under long grass. It also makes narrow tunnels just under the soil surface. This vole feeds mainly on grass, but it is a nuisance in young plantations because it nibbles the soft bark of the sapling trees. Active mostly at night but also by day, it is caught in large numbers by owls and other birds of prey.

The bank vole, distinguished by its brighter, browner coat and longer tail, prefers shrubby areas and hedgerows and never ventures far into the open grassland. Unlike the field vole, it often climbs bushes to eat fruits and insects. Rose hips are among the bank vole's favourite fruits, but it eats only the outer flesh: a naked cluster of pips shows that a bank vole has been at work.

You will not see moles very often because they spend almost all their time eating earthworms under the ground. They always let us know that they are there, however, by pushing up piles of soil here and there – the familiar mole hills. This soil comes from the mole's extensive tunnel system, which it excavates with its massive, shovel-like front feet. You might be lucky enough to see one of the hills being made. The mole uses its head for this and you might even see it push its head right out. The piles of soil soon collapse, especially in wet weather. Do not confuse them with ant-hills, which are also common in fields and meadows. These ant-hills are permanent mounds and usually covered with grass and other plants.

Invading Scrub

In the absence of grazing by rabbits and other animals the grasslands are rapidly colonized by shrubs. Hawthorn and birch are among the

Above: Grasslands undergo huge changes when grazing stops. Tall grasses swamp the smaller ones and within a few years bushes begin to appear – having grown from seeds brought by birds or by the wind. This chalk hillside was open grassland only a few years ago.

first to appear, closely followed by brambles and wild roses. Sallow is quick to invade the damper soils, while privet soon springs up on the dry soils of the chalk. If there is an overgrown grassland near you, make a count of the number of different kinds of shrubs. The shrubs shade out most of the low-growing flowering plants, and the whole area may gradually become woodland if people do not intervene and remove the scrub. Changes like these can take place very quickly, as happened when most of the rabbit population in Britain was killed by the myxomatosis outbreak in the 1950s.

Some of our older hedgerows came into existence by a similar process of succession. They sprang up on the no man's land between neighbouring farms or villages and gradually came to serve as boundaries. Other old hedges are the strips of trees and bushes left behind as boundaries when woodlands were cleared for agriculture. But most of today's hedges are much newer, having been planted during the last 200 years to enclose much of the original common land. These newer hedges generally have fewer kinds of shrubs in them and they tend to be much straighter than rambling ancient hedgerows.

SOME HEDGEROW FLOWERS

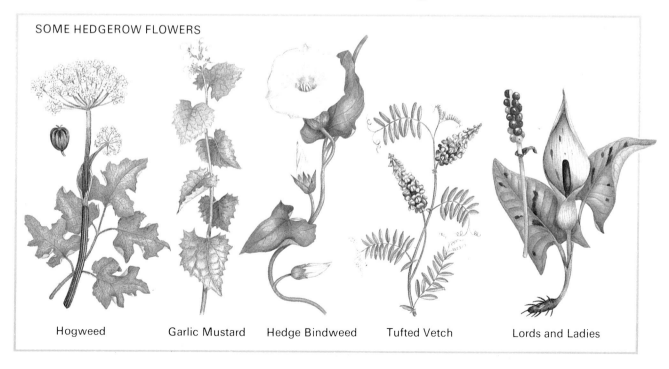

Hogweed   Garlic Mustard   Hedge Bindweed   Tufted Vetch   Lords and Ladies

A Hedgerow Year

Spring

This flower-rich spring hedgerow is dominated by gorse bushes with their brilliant yellow flowers. The cow parsley is beginning to open and there are buttercup and stitchwort flowers nearer to the ground. Lots of bees are already busy at the flowers. Small oaks and elms are putting out their leaves, while the wild rose is already shooting rapidly into the air. In late spring it will be covered with delicate pink flowers. The dense growth of the hedge is ideal for nesting birds, such as blackbirds, dunnocks and whitethroats. Linnets may also nest in the gorse bushes. Watch carefully for the comings and goings of the birds, but never poke about to find their nests. This hedge is obviously trimmed regularly to keep it low but, if done in winter, this does not affect the birds.

Summer

This ancient hedgerow, seen here in its full summer glory, contains many different kinds of shrubs and herbaceous plants. On the left you can see the wayfaring tree, one of our earliest-fruiting species. You can already see the oval and rather flattened berries beginning to ripen. They are black when fully ripe. Such a hedge will be alive with insects. Search for them by looking for tell-tale signs of chewed leaves: sometimes you will find that whole branches have been stripped by caterpillars. It is just the place to watch for a cuckoo in early summer, swooping to and fro in search of its favourite food – hairy caterpillars. Songthrushes, chaffinches and many other birds will nest in a thick hedge like this. Use your notebook to keep a record of the birds and other animals you find.

Autumn

Autumn is the season for fruit, and in a good year the hedges are weighed down with a colourful assortment of berries and other fruits. This hedgerow is covered with deep red haws, the fruits of the hawthorn. Other common fruits that you might find are the bright orange-red hips of the wild rose, the small black fruits of the dogwood and the wild privet, and of course the delicious blackberries which you can eat and enjoy. But remember that many of the hedgerow fruits are poisonous – even if the birds eat them without harm it does not mean that you can eat them as well. Try to keep a record of which kinds of birds eat which kinds of fruits. Watch the leaves change colour and fall as autumn progresses. You can then see how many birds nested in the hedge and examine the old nests.

Winter

This straight hedgerow, standing leafless in the winter, consists mainly of hawthorn and was obviously planted specifically as a field boundary (see page 23). Most of the haws have been stripped by the birds, but a few remain. As well as our resident thrushes and other fruit-eating birds, fieldfares and redwings from northern Europe arrive to feast on the hedgerow fruits in the winter. Some fruits ripen much earlier than others and are eaten first. Rose hips and the bright red garlands of black bryony berries are some of the latest to disappear. Many people think that a good berry crop indicates a hard winter on the way, but it really shows that the previous year's summer was a good one, for this is when the buds which eventually produced the fruits were formed.

Flowers of the Hedgerow

It is possible to estimate the age of an old hedge by counting the number of different kinds of trees and shrubs in a 30-metre stretch. As a very rough guide, you can say that there is one species for every 100 years of the hedge's life. This simple rule was discovered by Max Hooper after the study of hundreds of old hedges in Britain. It is best to count the species in several 30-metre stretches if possible and average the results. Look for large stumps in the hedge to prove that it is old rather than recently planted with lots of species.

Hedgerow Flowers

Whatever their origin, the hedgerows contain lots of wild flowers that enjoy shelter. Roadside hedges and verges are good places to see these flowers and some of them tell us the history of the hedge. Bluebells, wood anemones and dog's mercury, for example, indicate that the hedge was certainly once part of a wood.

Cow parsley and hogweed are two very common hedgerow umbellifers – plants that carry umbrella-like heads of small flowers. Cow parsley blooms in late spring and its very delicate white flowers have given it the alternative name of Queen Anne's lace. Hogweed blooms a little later and goes on for much of the summer. Its flowers are larger and its stems are much thicker and rougher than those of the cow parsley. Examine the hogweed's flower-heads for insects. Hundreds of different kinds of flies and beetles gather here to lap up the nectar. You can see the nectar yourself: it forms glistening beads in the centre of the little flowers. Do not muddle the hogweed with the strongly

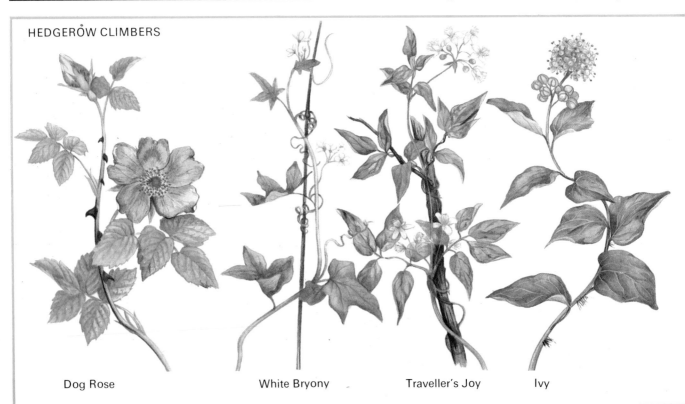

HEDGEROW CLIMBERS

Dog Rose   White Bryony   Traveller's Joy   Ivy

scented yarrow. This also has white flower heads, but the stalks do not all come from the same point as they do in the umbels. Yarrow also has very ferny leaves.

Look for the strange flower spikes of the lords-and-ladies in spring. Their unpleasant smell attracts small flies, which crawl down the spikes and pollinate them. Very poisonous red berries develop later.

Hedgerow Climbers

You will find many climbing plants in the hedgerows and some of the commonest kinds are pictured below. They all have weak stems and need the support of the hedgerow trees and shrubs to grow tall. Try to work out how each kind of climber actually climbs. Examine the tiny hooked prickles on the stems of the goosegrass, or cleavers, that smothers many rural hedgerows – and also clings tightly to your clothes. Black bryony, unrelated to the white bryony shown below, twines around its supports. It is not very obvious in the summer, but when the leaves fall in autumn you can see its brilliant red

berries festooning the bare twigs. You might wonder why these tempting berries are not snapped up by the birds. The truth is that they do not taste pleasant to the birds until well into the winter when their juice has lost its bitter tang. Although birds can eat these berries, they are very poisonous to people and you must leave them alone.

Above: The speckled bush cricket is very common among hedgerow nettles and brambles. The brown 'saddle' of this male is formed from its very short wings.

Caterpillar Hide-and-Seek

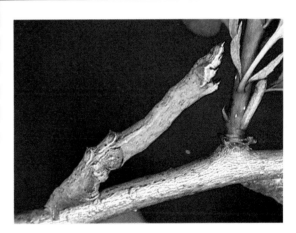

Many hedgerow caterpillars, such as this early thorn caterpillar, are extremely well camouflaged. They look just like twigs and you must look very hard to find them. Even the birds are fooled for much of the time, as long as the caterpillars keep still. They usually feed at night, when the birds are asleep.

Honeysuckle   Bramble

Slugs and Snails

The Robin's Pincushion

Gall

Grub

Hand lens

Examine wild roses in late summer for the fluffy red or orange growths known as robin's pincushions. These are galls, caused by the presence of tiny insect grubs in the plant's stems or leaves. Cut open a gall with a sharp knife and you will see the grubs, each in its own little chamber. If you collect a gall in early spring and keep it in a jam jar you will be able to see the adult insects come out. They are called gall wasps. Release them on the wild roses and you will get a new crop of pincushions in the summer. Look for other kinds of galls. They occur on many kinds of plants, but oaks are best.

Above: Snails like damp conditions and usually hide away in dry weather, but these striped snails cluster on plant stems in the summer drought. Their shells are sealed with hardened slime to keep in moisture.

Hedgerow Insects

Huge numbers of insects live in the hedge. Many feed on the leaves and flowers, but some are carnivorous and attack the plant-eaters. Search a short stretch of hedgerow carefully and you will be amazed at how many insects you find. Look for tell-tale holes in leaves to show you where caterpillars have been feeding. You will still have to look carefully for the caterpillars because many of them are wonderfully camouflaged. You can keep the caterpillars at home, as described on page 59. Some caterpillars like to bury themselves before turning into pupae, so put a layer of moist peat in the bottom of the cage.

Most of the caterpillars feeding on the shrubs will turn into moths. You can often find the adult moths resting on the hedgerow leaves and twigs by day or you can shake the branches to see what falls out. If you walk along the hedgerow at night you will see some of the moths in flight or feeding at the flowers. By day, of course, it is the butterflies that feed at the flowers. Bramble flowers are particularly attractive to them. Several of the butterflies illustrated on page 61 can be seen in the hedgerow.

Listen for the songs of the bush-crickets — short chirps or prolonged buzzing sounds. These insects are related to the grasshoppers but they have much longer antennae and sing by rubbing their wings together. Unlike grasshoppers, they are often active at night.

Slugs and Snails

Hedgerows, especially those with ditches beside them, make fine homes for slugs and snails. These animals revel in the damp conditions at the bottom of the hedge and grow fat on the decaying leaves. The best way to find them at work is to explore the hedgerow with a torch at night, but you can also find plenty of slugs and snails crawling around after a summer shower in the daytime. Look on roadside verges just after the grass has been cut, for the animals like to feed on the dying grass. Large black slugs are very common here. They may be 15 centimetres long, but if you prod one you will see it shrink

The Spider's Web

Spiders' webs look beautiful when laden with dew or frost in the early morning, but what is really remarkable is the speed and precision with which the webs are built. Search the hedgerow carefully to find a spider at work. Some of the stages are illustrated here. First of all the spider forms a bridge thread across the top (1), then it completes the outer framework (2). The 'spokes' are put in place next (3), and then a central platform (4). The spider finishes off with the sticky spiral threads which actually trap flies and other insects. Some spiders construct new webs each day.

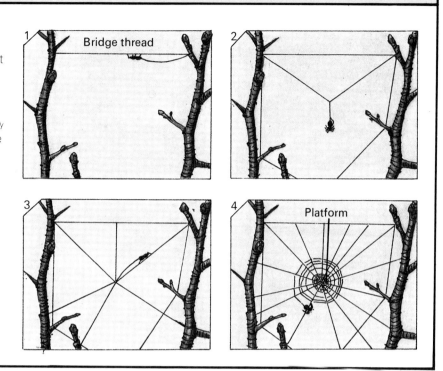

to a black blob and sway from side to side. Notice how sticky your fingers are after touching the slug. The sticky slime helps to keep the slug moist and also protects it from its enemies. You might also see large brown or orange slugs, especially in southern areas. These are just varieties of the large black slug.

The hedgerow snails include many of the banded snails that live on open grassland. Look also for the Kentish snail, whose creamy white shell usually has a reddish brown area near the opening. Watch how the snails glide smoothly over the grass, leaving a trail of slime behind them. The slime helps to lubricate their passage. Put a slug or snail in a jam jar and observe it through the glass. Notice the muscles rippling in the foot as the animal glides along.

Lurking Spiders

The abundant insect life of the hedge provides plenty of food for spiders. Keep a watch on a hedge in the autumn to see just how many spiders live there and wait for insects to land in their webs. The webs show

up clearly when laced with dew on autumn mornings. There are many kinds of webs apart from the orb-web seen above. Most numerous are the little hammock webs. These are normally flat or domed, but often sag when laden with dew. Look underneath the web for the little spider. *Linyphia triangularis* is the commonest. It has a row of dark triangles along its back. Look above the hammock to see a network of 'scaffolding'. Small insects bump into these silken threads and fall on to the hammock. The spider then bites them through the web before they can escape. The web is not sticky, but the insects get their feet tangled in it.

Examine the plants by the side of the hedge in the summer for the silken tents of the nursery-web spider. The mother spider fixes her ball of eggs to a plant and then spins the tent over them for protection. She usually sits on the web until the eggs hatch and, as long as you do not make any sudden movements, it is quite easy to watch her. She will scurry away when you get close to see the egg-ball, but she will soon come back. If the eggs have hatched

Hedgerow Mammals

What's in a Nest?

Broken eggs

Old abandoned nest

Nail

Card

Nesting materials

Hedgerow birds build new nests each year and you can safely take down the old nests to examine them in the autumn. Put them into plastic bags with a little moth-proofer for a while to kill the fleas in them. Then you can pull the nests to pieces to see what they are made of. You can even make a collection of old nests if you have room. Put them on stout card or in shoeboxes. Label with the type of nest and where and when you found it. Never take nests unless you are sure they have been abandoned.

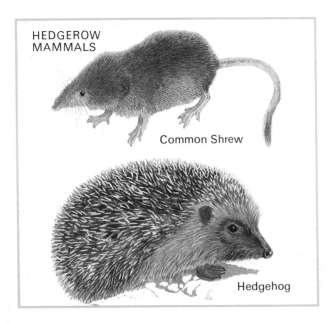

HEDGEROW MAMMALS

Common Shrew

Hedgehog

you might see hundreds of tiny babies in the tent, although they soon scatter to begin their own lives. This kind of spider is a hunter, chasing small insects instead of making a web to trap them.

The Prickly Hedgehog

As dusk falls on the hedgerow the hedgehog wakes up for its nightly ramble. The best way to find it is to listen for its grunting and scuffling as it searches for slugs and other small animals in the leaf litter at the bottom of the hedge. You can then use your torch to pick out this fascinating little mammal. It does not mind the light and may well sit and watch you for a while before ambling off surprisingly quickly. Notice its pointed snout, which helps it to sniff out its food. If the hedgehog is really alarmed it may roll into a prickly ball. This protects it from most of its enemies, but not from motor cars and many hedgehogs can be seen squashed on the roads. It is difficult to discover the hedgehog's footprints in the rough ground of the hedge, but you can sometimes find its long black droppings, usually full of beetle wing cases. Do not forget that hedgehogs go to sleep for the winter: summer and autumn are the best times for looking for them.

The shrews are closely related to the hedgehog. The common shrew is very common in the hedgerow, where it feeds on a wide range of small animals. Listen carefully for its high-pitched squeaks. It is active day and night, but you will not see it very often because it keeps to dense cover.

The Farmer's Fields

All farmland is artificial, but some of the fields are more natural than others. The rough pastures of the uplands are not touched by the plough and the steep slopes are covered with native grasses and other plants which have spread over the hills since the trees disappeared. These rough grazing lands may be divided by stone walls, but are often wide open and the sheep can roam over vast areas.

The lower slopes and most lowland areas are regularly cultivated and their vegetation is far from natural. The pastures where cattle graze may look natural, but most of them have been sown with special mixtures of grass seed to provide the best grasses for the cattle. Native plants gradually invade the fields and the grazing quality gradually falls until the farmer re-seeds the land with the cultivated grasses. Hay meadows are usually treated in the same way. Here the grasses are allowed to grow up and flower in the summer before being cut for hay. Two or even three crops may be taken in some years, especially if the fields are heavily manured or fertilized. Many meadows are now cut for silage. The grass is cut while still green and stored in special pits where it is turned into a sweet 'cake' which the cattle enjoy during the winter.

Clover and lucerne are often sown with the grasses for hay and silage, but you will not find many other flowers in modern hay meadows or leys. There are, however, a number of ancient meadows which have never been ploughed or treated with fertilizer and which still support a wealth of wild flowers. Such meadows are particularly common on hillsides and the best examples can be seen in the Alps.

Food from the Fields

The cereals are the most important of our field crops. They are all large grasses with starch-filled edible grains. Four major cereals are shown on the left below. Watch out for them when you are out and about in the countryside. Look for other kinds of cereals and other food crops as well. Some of these are grown for us to eat while others provide food for cattle and other animals. Many crops are grown for the oil in their seeds. Examples include sunflowers, linseed, lupins and rape. The latter turns many fields brilliant yellow in the spring.

Below: This agricultural scene has been created entirely by people and their animals. Crops are grown in most of the fields, but cattle graze on the rougher grassland in the foreground.

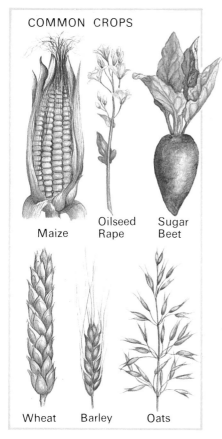

COMMON CROPS

Maize

Oilseed Rape

Sugar Beet

Wheat

Barley

Oats

Insect Projects

An Insect Survey

Use a beating tray like that shown on page 38 to study the insect life of a stretch of hedgerow. Hundreds of different kinds of insect live in the hedge in the summer but you don't have to be able to identify them all to carry out this simple project. Beat each different kind of shrub in turn and note the number of *different kinds* of insect that you find on each. Beat as many different kinds of bush as you can, and record the numbers of insects you find in your notebook. Make sketches of each kind of insect, or write brief descriptions, so that you will recognize the insects when you meet them again. Remember to shake the insects back on to the bush afterwards. You can continue the project all through the summer, but keep a separate tally for each kind of bush. Try this project on trees in the woods as well.

Recording Results

Make a simple graph of your results, showing the number of *different kinds* of insect found on each kind of bush or tree. You will probably get a result looking something like the one shown here. You can see that the oak has more kinds of insect living on it than any other kind of tree. The sycamore and the horse chestnut have very few insects living on them in Britain. Can you think why this should be?

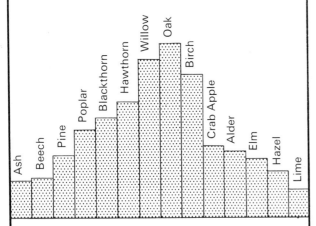

Above: This graph compares the numbers of insect species that you might find on various kinds of tree. Oak, willow and birch provide food for the greatest variety of insects.

The Natural History of a Cowpat

You probably steer well clear of cowpats in the fields, but a good naturalist will always have a look at them. There is always something to be seen on and around the dung. The most obvious animals, especially on fresh dung, are the furry yellow dung-flies that fly up in clouds as you approach. Dung-flies play a very important role in nature. They lay their eggs in the cowpats and their maggots gradually eat their way through the dung. Think what life would be like without any animals to eat up all the dung!

Many beetles also feed on the cowpats. Use a stick or an old knife to probe for them. Turn over old and dried cowpats to see if any beetles are lurking beneath them. Select a fresh cowpat and visit it every day. Record the visible changes in your notebook, together with drawings or brief descriptions of the insects you see. You can also collect examples of the insects and try to identify them when you get home. Note how the cowpat gradually shrinks as it is used up. Most of the dung beetles feed and grow up in the cowpat itself, but some species bury the dung before eating it or laying eggs on it. The most famous of these are the scarabs, which roll balls of dung around as they search for suitable burial sites. None of the scarabs live in Britain, but you might see some in southern Europe.

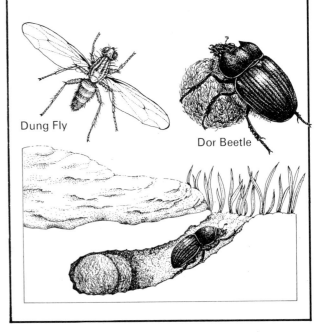

Dung Fly

Dor Beetle

SEASHORE, PONDS AND STREAMS

The seashore is the boundary between the land and the
sea and is always changing as the waves wear away
cliffs in some places and build up huge banks of sand
and shingle in others. Animals living on the shore have
to be able to withstand the battering of the waves,
which cover them twice every day.
Ponds and streams are part of the vital water cycle,
which takes rainwater back to the sea.

Explore these watery habitats and their wildlife. Find
out about the intriguing behaviour of the aggressive
little stickleback and discover how to tempt a crab
from its hiding place. Learn how to recognize
waterside birds and the shells of the seashore.

A Walk by the Sea

Our seaside walk starts on a cliff-top high above a sandy bay. As you walk over the headland, keep to the narrow path for your own safety, but stop every now and then to look at the view and to examine the rocks. There is an amazing variety of rocks around the British coastline, including sandstone, limestones and the granites pictured here. Limestones include the chalk rocks which produce many of our famous white cliffs. Some of the rocks are more than 1000 million years old, while others have barely seen one million years pass by.

Many of the rocks contain fossils, which are the remains of long-dead plants and animals. Limestones are particularly rich in fossils, including the remains of sea shells, while chalk is made almost entirely of the shells of microscopic sea creatures called forams. The existence of all these marine fossils proves that the rocks were formed under the sea, and that the Earth has undergone immense changes.

You can see some of these changes in progress at the foot of the headland. Here the sea is at war with the land and you can see the waves battering the rocks and breaking pieces away. It will be millions of years before the cliffs disappear, but they will crumble into the sea eventually. Their fragments will be compressed into new rocks on the sea bed and, far into the future, they will be pushed up again to form fresh land.

Look down along the coast from your cliff-top position. If the tide is out you may be able to see that the higher parts of the shore are shingle while the lower parts are sandy. This is because the incoming waves can throw pebbles far up the beach but the backwash is not strong enough to carry them down again. You may also see rows of wooden or concrete groynes sticking out into the sea. These protect the beaches of resorts. Notice how the sand or shingle builds up on one side of each groyne. Waves always come in at an angle, and sweep the sand and shingle along the beach rather than straight up. Without

The Seashore Code

1. Respect the plants and animals living on the shore.
2. Never throw rubbish of any kind into the water: it can cause pollution and harm wildlife.
3. Test the bottom carefully when investigating plantlife or paddling. Keep away from thick mud.
4. Always find out the times of high tide. Don't get trapped by incoming waves.

A Walk by the Sea

the groynes, the sand and shingle would be swept away from one end of the beach and piled up at the other end. This process is called longshore drift.

As you continue your walk across the cliffs take a good look at the many beautiful flowers that manage to survive the windy conditions and the salty spray. The pictures on the right will help you identify some of them. Thrift, also known as sea pink, turns the cliff-tops and ledges pink in summer. You will probably see and hear many sea birds squabbling over seats on the narrow ledges. You might find them nesting on the ledges in the spring, but don't be tempted to get too near the edge to look at them.

After a while, the cliffs begin to get lower and the path drops down to a small sandy bay. You have left the hard rocks of the headland and moved on to an outcrop of softer rock. The waves have been able to eat into this and have carved out the bay. Here the beach is protected by headlands on each side. The bay is lapped by gentle waves which wash in sand but cannot bring in the heavier shingle, so a fine sandy beach has been formed. Behind it, there are a number of dunes – ridges of sand piled up by the wind. Those nearest to the sea are still quite loose, but those further back have been fixed by clumps of tough marram grass and other plants, such as sea holly. The roots of these plants bind the sand together and stop it from being blown about too much. Still further back, the dunes may be covered with turf, heather or other small shrubs.

A small stream runs down to the beach at low tide, but when the tide comes in again the water surges up the stream-bed and over the banks. Fine mud gradually builds up in this area and forms a saltmarsh. Many interesting plants and animals live here and the marsh is an important feeding ground for geese and wading birds, especially in winter.

Tides sweep in twice every day. They are caused by the gravitational pull of the sun and the moon, and this pull varies as the Earth rotates on its axis and the moon rotates around the Earth. High-tide level is therefore not the same every day. Every two weeks at

COMMON COASTAL FLOWERS

Sea Holly

Sea Pea

Thrift

Sea Purslane

Salty Problems

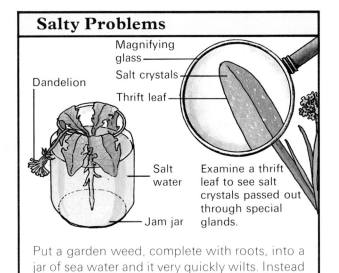

Magnifying glass

Salt crystals

Thrift leaf

Dandelion

Salt water

Jam jar

Examine a thrift leaf to see salt crystals passed out through special glands.

Put a garden weed, complete with roots, into a jar of sea water and it very quickly wilts. Instead of the roots sucking in water, the salty water draws the sap out of the plant. Seaside plants have a very strong sap and can take in water from their salty surroundings.

Glasswort

Sea Lavender

Sea Kale

Seablite

Hottentot Fig

Yellow Horned-poppy

Sea Campion

Right: The estuarine reach of a river, where it joins the sea, is often very muddy. You can see this very easily at low tide. The banks are flooded by the highest tides and the soil is rather salty. These areas are known as salt-marshes and they are often dissected by muddy channels which carry the water away as the tide falls. Only specialized, salt-tolerant plants can grow here, including the thrift which makes the marsh on the right so colourful.

A Rocky Seashore

the time of new and full moons, there are especially strong tides called spring tides. In the days following a spring tide the high-water mark gets progressively lower, and then rises again towards the next spring tide.

Rocky Shores

As we have seen on our short walk, there are several different kinds of seashore and each type supports its own kinds of wildlife. Let's start with a rocky shore.

As the tide goes out you will see that the rocks are clothed with seaweeds in most places. There are many different kinds of seaweeds. Most of them are brown, but there are also green ones and red ones. Select a patch of seaweed growing on the upper half of the shore and note the time at which it is covered by the incoming tide. How many hours pass before it is uncovered again? The higher up the shore your seaweeds are growing, the shorter the period of immersion and the longer the exposure to the air. Different seaweeds can survive different

amounts of exposure, and therefore are found growing in distinct zones on the shore.

The green seaweeds can survive plenty of exposure to air and rain and can grow near the top of the beach. Look for them also where streams of fresh water trickle over the shore. Sea lettuce is a very common species, but the most abundant of the green seaweeds is *Enteromorpha*. This is sometimes called sea grass because it waves about like grass when covered by the tide, but when uncovered it collapses and forms a very slippery mat.

You will also find the brown channelled wrack at the top of the shore, the upper zone. Look carefully at its branching fronds to see the narrow channels which give the plant its name. These hold water and help the plant to survive in the air. There may be some days when these upper-shore seaweeds are not reached by the tide at all, although they are probably splashed by spray every day.

The middle part of the beach is clothed mainly with brown seaweeds, such as toothed wrack and bladder wrack, but even here the

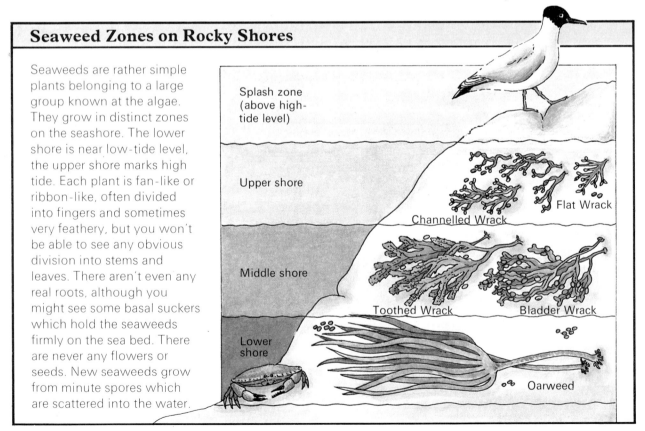

Seaweed Zones on Rocky Shores

Seaweeds are rather simple plants belonging to a large group known at the algae. They grow in distinct zones on the seashore. The lower shore is near low-tide level, the upper shore marks high tide. Each plant is fan-like or ribbon-like, often divided into fingers and sometimes very feathery, but you won't be able to see any obvious division into stems and leaves. There aren't even any real roots, although you might see some basal suckers which hold the seaweeds firmly on the sea bed. There are never any flowers or seeds. New seaweeds grow from minute spores which are scattered into the water.

Splash zone (above high-tide level)

Upper shore

Middle shore

Lower shore

Flat Wrack

Channelled Wrack

Toothed Wrack

Bladder Wrack

Oarweed

species are clearly zoned. The toothed wrack, which you can recognize by its saw-like edges, will not grow if exposed to the air for more than about six hours at a time, and so it is confined to a zone below mid-tide level. Bladder wrack, recognized by the air-filled bladders on its fronds, can withstand more exposure than the toothed wrack, but not as much as the channelled wrack. It therefore occupies a zone between the two.

The largest seaweeds around our coasts are the brown oarweeds, such as the sea belt, that grow in dense 'forests' just below low-water mark. You can sometimes see these seaweeds just poking out of the water at the lowest tides, but you will more often find them thrown up on the beach after a storm. The sea belt may be as much as nine metres long.

Red seaweeds are generally rather small and delicate and they cannot survive out of water for very long. Look for them on the lowest parts of the shore and also in rock pools. Many of them are coated with chalky material and become white when they die.

The Strand Line

Each tide brings in an assortment of seaweed, shells and other debris. Much of this is left in the strand line at high-water mark. You will find an amazing variety of small animals amongst the debris. Seagulls and other birds know this as well: watch them scurrying along the strand line and turning over the seaweed as they search for food.

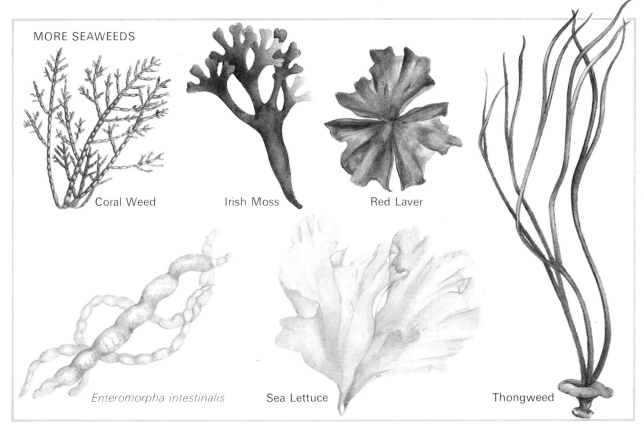

MORE SEAWEEDS

Coral Weed

Irish Moss

Red Laver

Enteromorpha intestinalis

Sea Lettuce

Thongweed

Animals on the Rocks

Animals on the Rocks

The seaweeds provide food and shelter for many animals. Try searching through a patch of weeds at low tide. It won't take long to find the periwinkles – small sea snails that browse on the seaweeds. Look out also for the attractive top shells, shaped just like old-fashioned spinning tops. Put some of the shells into a bucket or dish of sea water so you can see the animals crawling about.

You will find the conical shells of the common limpet all over the rocks. A sudden knock with a stone may dislodge the animal, but otherwise it is almost impossible to remove it. Even the full force of the waves crashing on to the rocks cannot overcome the limpet's astonishing grip, but when completely submerged the limpet relaxes its grip and wanders off to feed. Although its shell is not coiled, the limpet is just another sea snail and, like all snails, it has a tongue like a strip of sandpaper. It uses this tongue to scrape small seaweeds from the rocks. In places where there are lots of limpets the rocks are almost bare. After feeding, the limpet always returns to the same resting place, and gradually wears a circular groove in the rock. Each limpet fits its home extremely well.

Browsing Periwinkles

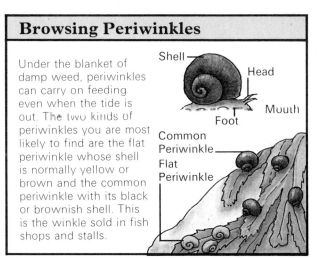

Under the blanket of damp weed, periwinkles can carry on feeding even when the tide is out. The two kinds of periwinkles you are most likely to find are the flat periwinkle whose shell is normally yellow or brown and the common periwinkle with its black or brownish shell. This is the winkle sold in fish shops and stalls.

In some places the waves are a little too strong for seaweeds to survive on the rocks, and this is where the barnacles take over. Their conical white shells are sometimes so numerous that you cannot put a pencil point between them. The barnacles can live in such dense colonies because the tides are always bringing in fresh food supplies. Young barnacles float in the water for a while before settling down on the rocks. If they are to survive they must land in an area where they are submerged long enough for them to get sufficient food, but they must also be exposed

Painting Limpets

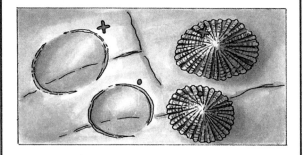

Look for limpets at low tide and mark a few with blobs of quick-drying paint. Put similar marks on the rock nearby. You will find the limpets in exactly the same spot the next day, but if you could watch them when the tide is in you would see that they move away to feed on algae (as above). Notice the scars on the rock, formed by friction between the shells and the rock.

Observing Barnacles

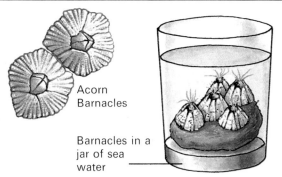

Acorn Barnacles

Barnacles in a jar of sea water

Look for some barnacles on a small stone that you can put into a dish of sea water. You can then see these strange little animals at work. Under the water they open their shells and push out feathery limbs which rhythmically comb the water for food particles. Return them to the place you found them after the experiment.

to the air for a few hours each day. Many young barnacles fail to find suitable places, but their fate is not left entirely to chance. The youngsters are attracted by the scent of existing colonies and they tend to settle near them – in places which are obviously suitable for barnacle growth.

The dark blue shells of mussels often cluster on the same rocks as the barnacles, attached by bunches of strong threads. Like the barnacles, they depend on the tides and waves to bring their food. The shells open slightly when they are under water and, just like the cockles, the mussels suck in streams of water and filter microscopic plants and other food from it.

If you examine mussel and barnacle colonies you might well see some of the sea snails called dog whelks. Their shells are generally yellow or white, often with brown or black bands, and they are extremely thick – a necessity if they are to survive the pounding of the rough water around the rocks. Unlike the periwinkles and top shells, the dog whelks are flesh-eaters. Look at empty mussel shells thrown up on the beach: many will have a small hole near the apex (tip), showing where a dog whelk got to work. Barnacles are also

COMMON BIVALVES

Common Cockle

Common Mussel

Banded Wedge Shell

Common Piddock

Queen Scallop

Thin Tellin

Large Razor Shell

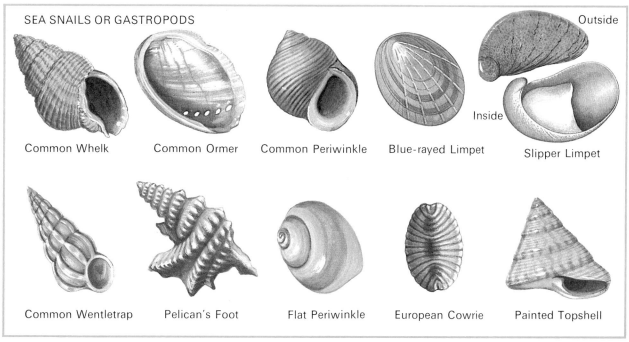

SEA SNAILS OR GASTROPODS

Common Whelk

Common Ormer

Common Periwinkle

Blue-rayed Limpet

Outside

Inside

Slipper Limpet

Common Wentletrap

Pelican's Foot

Flat Periwinkle

European Cowrie

Painted Topshell

Rock Crevices

Tempting a Crab

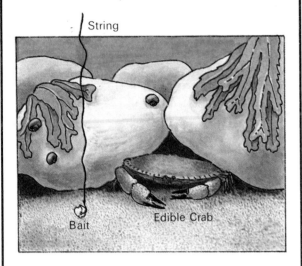

String

Bait

Edible Crab

Try tempting out a crab with a piece of meat or fish – perhaps a dead crab or starfish from the strand line. Tie the food to a piece of string and dangle it by a crevice in the rocks. If your crab comes out to investigate, let it grab the food with its great claws: it may hold on so tightly that you can lift it out.

eaten by these carnivorous snails, but they are less nutritious than mussels and the dog whelks feeding in a barnacle colony tend to be smaller than those feeding on mussels. They usually have paler shells as well.

Rock Crevices

Rock crevices are good places to explore. Many animals hide here to escape the drying action of the sun and wind. High on the shore you will find the woodlouse-like sea slater, which comes out at night to feed on decaying seaweed and other rubbish. Lower down you may find various kinds of crabs. They venture out on dull days, but scuttle rapidly back into their crevices if they see you. Crabs are greedy scavengers and find it hard to resist the smell of food. Try tempting one out into the open and watch its curious sideways walk. Notice its stalked eyes and quivering antennae.

While exploring the crevices you will probably see some blobs of red jelly. They don't look much like animals, but they are sea

anemones safely tucked up until the tide returns. They are beautiful animals, but to see their flower-like beauty you need to investigate the rocks just below low-tide level. Here, if the water is clear, you will see the animals unfolded and waving their slender arms or tentacles. But don't be misled by their flower-like appearance: the anemones are death-traps for fishes and other small animals. The tentacles are clothed with hundreds of minute stings which are fired

Starfish Movement

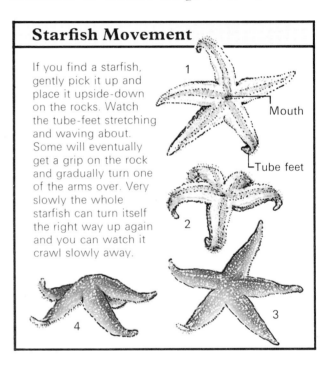

If you find a starfish, gently pick it up and place it upside-down on the rocks. Watch the tube-feet stretching and waving about. Some will eventually get a grip on the rock and gradually turn one of the arms over. Very slowly the whole starfish can turn itself the right way up again and you can watch it crawl slowly away.

1

Mouth

Tube feet

2

3

4

Dog Whelks

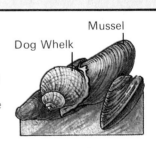

Dog Whelk

Mussel

Dog whelks use their rough tongues to drill through the shells of mussels, and then rasp out the soft flesh. The tongue then carries the rasped-out food into the dog whelk's mouth. No drilling is needed for the barnacles: the dog whelk merely forces back the small chalky plates at the top of the shell to get at the animal inside.

Common Dog Whelk

into any animal that brushes against the anemone. Small animals are quickly paralysed and then pulled into the anemone's mouth. You can watch the process by tying a small piece of meat or fish to a length of cotton and dangling it in the anemone's tentacles. These will immediately coil around the food and drag or push it into the mouth. It all happens very quickly.

The clear water around low-tide level is a superb place for observing those animals that can't stay out of the water for long. Here you can watch shrimps and prawns darting about in company with various small fishes, and you can also find many prickly sea urchins. Be careful not to tread on these animals when paddling, because their spines can make your feet very sore. On some of the softer rocks the urchins carve out little hollows for themselves and stay there permanently.

Starfishes of various kinds find plenty of other animals to eat in the shallows. Pick up a starfish and look at the underside: the arms are covered with little suckers called tube-feet. The starfish uses these to cling to the

rocks and to clamber over the surface. These powerful suckers are also used when feeding on cockles and other bivalves. They are so strong that they can pull the two halves of the shell apart: the starfish can then feed on the soft body inside.

Fascinating Rock Pools

Waves and the stones that they carry wear away some parts of the rocks more quickly than others. When the tide goes out each of these hollows remains full of water and is transformed into a natural aquarium. Here you can watch all kinds of seashore animals going about their lives just as if the tide were in. It is usually easier to watch animals in a pool than at low-water mark: there are no waves lapping around them, and you also have more time because the pools may be exposed for several hours. At low-water mark you have only a few minutes before the tide turns and comes in again.

Rock pools often have pink linings, produced by small red seaweeds whose flat fronds are encrusted with lime. Numerous

Above: Hermit crabs have long soft bodies, which they protect by taking up residence in empty shells. As they grow, the crabs move house to larger shells. Right: A rock pool with clumps of mussels and attendant dog whelks, a sea anemone in the middle, and a sea urchin which has camouflaged itself with small stones.

Rock Pools

sea snails browse on these and other seaweeds. Look out for shells moving across the bottom rather faster than normal. These will contain hermit crabs which protect their soft bodies by occupying empty snail shells. Look carefully, too, for small prawns on the bottom of the pools. They are not easy to see because they are almost transparent, but a pattern of red dots and streaks may give away their position. The chameleon prawn, which has a strongly arched back and is much smaller than the common prawn, can actually change colour to match sandy or weedy backgrounds in the pools.

Sea anemones flourish in rock pools because they are always underwater and can feed all day instead of spending half their time folded inwards to prevent themselves drying out. Look out for the snakelocks anemone. Its body is greenish brown, but the tentacles are lighter green and usually marked with red and white. The tentacles cannot be pulled right into the body and this anemone cannot survive on rocks which are exposed to the air.

Looking into a rock pool is not always easy, especially on a sunny day when there are many surface reflections. One way to solve

Observing Rock Pools

You can make a simple but effective viewer from a small plastic bucket or large yoghurt pot, a sheet of stretch plastic and a rubber band. Cut the bottom from the bucket or yoghurt pot and stretch the plastic over it. Fix firmly with the rubber band. Push the bottom of the bucket into the water and look through it.

Cut out the bottom and stretch plastic film over it.

Rubber band

Old bucket

this problem is to wear a diving mask. Or make a viewing screen as described above. If neither of these methods is possible, you can rig up some sort of sunshade to keep the sun's rays away from the pool. A small aquarium net will be useful for catching prawns and other small creatures. Tip them into a dish of sea water so that you can see them properly. Don't leave the dish in the sun, and remember to return the animals to the pool after you have looked at them.

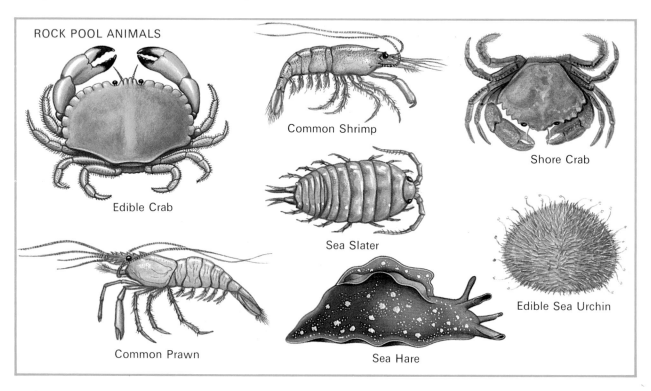

ROCK POOL ANIMALS

Common Shrimp

Shore Crab

Edible Crab

Sea Slater

Edible Sea Urchin

Common Prawn

Sea Hare

Life on the Sandy Shore

When the tide goes out over a sandy shore it leaves a blank sheet of sand. There aren't even any seaweeds, for they can't anchor themselves to the shifting sand. But the shore isn't really lifeless: if the top 30 centimetres of sand could be spirited away you would find a thick carpet of wriggling bodies. These animals burrow into the sand when the tide recedes and wait for it to return. The sand stays moist and the animals are in no danger of drying up.

Near the top of the beach you would find innumerable sand hoppers – small shrimp-like animals that live around high-water mark and come out to feed on the strand-line debris at night. Lower down on the shore you would find a few sea snails, together with shrimps and starfishes and a few sea urchins, but the great majority of the sand-dwellers are worms and bivalve molluscs. These molluscs, such as the cockles and razor shells and the beautiful pink tellins, have shells consisting of two valves hinged along one edge. They burrow through the sand with the aid of a muscular foot, and they move up to feed at the surface of the sand when the tide is in.

You might wonder what all these thousands of animals find to eat on the bare sand, but the tide actually washes in more than enough food for them. When the tide is in, the sea bed receives a constant rain of debris in the form of fragments of plants and dead animals and animal droppings, and it is this debris that feeds the bulk of the sea-bed creatures. Collect a jar of water from the incoming waves and you will see just how much sediment it carries.

The lugworm merely swallows the sand and mud and digests any food in it, but other animals have rather more refined methods of collecting their food. They are known as filter feeders. Many of the worms wriggle to the surface of the sand when the tide comes in and then expand a crown of feathery tentacles which trap the falling sediment and waft it into the mouth. Often known as fan worms, from the shape of their crowns, many are beautifully and delicately coloured. Most of them live in tubes which they build from sand particles cemented together with slime from their bodies. You can sometimes see these tubes poking out of the sand at low tide, but the worms are then hunched up right down at the bottom.

You can watch the filter-feeding action of the bivalves quite easily if you can find a live cockle or tellin in the sand or mud of the lower shore. Put your cockle into a jam jar

Above: Look for the turnstone on rocky and weedy beaches in winter. It is well-named, for it uses its beak to flip over stones in search of food.

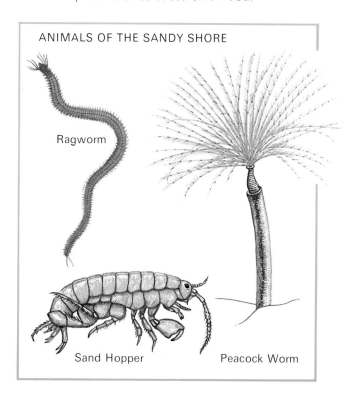

ANIMALS OF THE SANDY SHORE

Ragworm

Sand Hopper   Peacock Worm

Barren Shingle

Feeding a Cockle and a Tellin

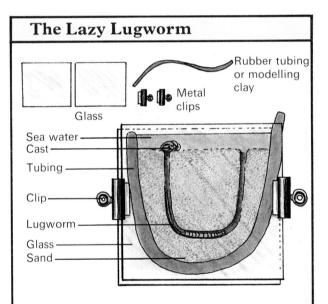

Eye-dropper

Jam jar

Sea water

Sand

Cockle

Jam jar

Tellin

Siphon

Put a cockle into a jam jar with enough sand for it to bury itself and then fill the jar with sea water. As the water clears you will see the cockle's two frilly breathing tubes or siphons just above the sand. Use a simple eye-dropper to squirt a few drops of gravy or soup just above the cockle and watch the food stream into one of the siphons. Put a tellin into another jar and watch its siphons hoovering up the sand. Notice that one of its siphons is much larger than the other.

Barren Shingle

Shingle beaches generally develop on exposed coasts, where the strong waves can hurl the stones high on the beach. You often find a ridge of very large stones right at the top of the beach, thrown there by storm waves during the highest tides. Very few animals can live in the shingle because they would be crushed as the stones tumble about, but you might find a few sea slaters around high-water mark. Water shortage is also a problem, because water drains away very quickly through the shingle. Seaweeds can't establish themselves on the rolling stones, but a few flowering plants manage to grow in the shingle just above high-water mark. Long roots reach down to the moisture and also anchor the plants securely in the moving

containing sand and sea water – see above. Let the water clear and you will see two frilly tubes just poking through the sand. These are the cockle's breathing tubes or siphons. Water is sucked in through one tube, passed over the gills, and pumped out through the other tube. The gills take oxygen from the water and also filter out any food particles and pass them to the mouth. The tellin feeds rather differently. One of its siphons is very long and is used rather like the hose of a vacuum cleaner to suck debris from the sea bed, but the water and debris is still filtered through the gills.

The bivalves themselves are eaten by starfishes and some flesh-eating snails. Like the rock-living dog whelks, these snails bore holes in the bivalve shells to get at the flesh inside. Keep an eye open for drilled shells on the beach. Oystercatchers and other wading birds also eat lots of bivalves. Watch the birds probing for them in the sand and mud: with binoculars, you might be able to see how they open the shells with their beaks.

The Lazy Lugworm

Glass

Metal clips

Rubber tubing or modelling clay

Sea water
Cast
Tubing
Clip
Lugworm
Glass
Sand

To make this mini-aquarium fit a strip of modelling clay or a length of rubber tubing between two pieces of glass (each about 25 cm square) so that they are about 1 cm apart. Use the clips to hold the glass firmly so that sand and sea water can be held in the U-shaped chamber. Put a lugworm on the surface and watch it make its L-shaped burrow. It will soon start to feed by sucking sand in through the mouth. This causes the tell-tale depression in the sand above it. Food particles in the sand are digested and the sand itself is later pushed out from the hind end to make worm casts on the surface.

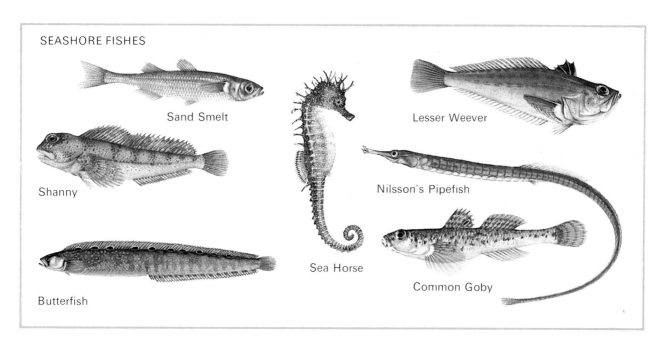

SEASHORE FISHES

Sand Smelt

Shanny

Butterfish

Sea Horse

Lesser Weever

Nilsson's Pipefish

Common Goby

Below: Most fishes go out with the tide. If you want to get a proper look at them you can use a shrimping net. Push it gently along the sand in the shallows; it will catch several of the fishes shown above, as well as numerous shrimps.

shingle. The sea sandwort forms bright green mats over the shingle in many places, while here and there you will find the beautiful sea pea and the yellow horned-poppy.

Birds of the Beaches

The most noticeable birds around the seashore are the gulls. You can see them even in busy resorts, gliding over the beaches and swooping down in noisy gangs in search of food. They are real scavengers and their strong beaks can deal with most kinds of food: they can even crack open the shells of crabs to get at the juicy meat inside. The birds pay great attention to the water's edge, where crabs and other small animals may be stranded, and they are quite likely to steal your sandwiches if you are not careful.

Keep your eyes open for the different kinds of gulls. Three are very common, but you might well see five or six different kinds. The herring gull is so common that it has become a pest in some places: it covers buildings with its droppings and also eats the eggs and nestlings of other birds on nature reserves. Its back is light to dark grey and its legs are usually pink. The lesser black-backed gull is similar, but a little smaller, and generally has a darker back. Its legs are usually yellow. The black-headed gull is another abundant

Seaside Birds

species. You can recognize it very easily in summer by its black head and wing-tips and its dark red beak. In the winter the head becomes white, with just a brownish patch behind the eye. All three kinds of gulls nest on the ground on dunes and saltmarshes, but the herring gull also nests on cliffs. The black-headed gull nests far inland as well as by the sea, and many of these gulls never actually see the sea in their lives. Look for them around rubbish dumps and reservoirs.

The terns are closely related to the gulls but they are much daintier birds, with pointed beaks and long, forked tails. Watch them fluttering just above the waves with their beaks pointing straight down as they look for fish. You might see them hover for a while and then plunge into the water to snatch up a fish. Terns lay their eggs on sand or shingle, without building any real nest.

Above: Rugged cliffs make excellent nesting sites for gulls and other sea birds because few enemies can reach them. Most of the gulls here are kittiwakes, whose nests are made with grass, mud and seaweed.

SEA BIRDS

male

female

Shelduck

Common Tern

female

male

Long-tailed Duck

dark-bellied form

light-bellied form

Brent Goose

Fulmar

winter

summer

British form

Scandinavian form

Guillemot

Lesser Black-backed Gull

Razorbill

To see some of the many other kinds of sea-birds you will have to visit wilder parts of the coastline. Many of these birds come ashore only in the spring breeding season and spend the rest of the year fishing out at sea, often very far away from land. These birds include gannets, guillemots, razorbills, and the comical puffins. They all like to breed on rugged cliffs, especially on small islands and other remote areas, and there may be many thousands of them nesting in a small area. These nesting colonies are best seen from out at sea and sight-seeing boat trips are often available from nearby harbours.

Wading birds flock to the shore at low tide to probe the mud and sand with their long beaks, hoping to find worms and shellfish. Use your binoculars (see page 111) to watch them feeding. Winter is the best time to see the waders because many species spend the summer on the Arctic tundra. Many ducks and geese also fly down from the north to spend the winter on our seashore.

The spring and autumn migration periods are especially exciting for the seashore bird-watcher, for this is when we see the passage migrants such as the curlew sandpiper and the little stint – birds which breed in the far north and then fly to Africa for the winter. They use the shores of western Europe as refuelling stops. But it is not only water birds that can be found on the coast during the migration periods. Many of the summer visitors to our fields and woodlands come from Africa and they find the shore a welcome resting place after their long sea crossings. They may feed around the shore for several days before flying on to look for inland nesting sites. These birds may also gather on the shore before leaving again in the autumn.

Continental form

Atlantic form

summer

winter

Cormorant

Puffin

Redshank

Ringed Plover

Little Ringed Plover

winter

summer

Oystercatcher

Turnstone

Gannet

A Walk by a River

The stream gleams as it flows over its bed of stones and gravel. The water is shallow in most places and banks of gravel break the surface in several spots. But here and there, especially on the outsides of the bends, there are some deeper pools. The water is clear and you can see small shoals of fishes darting about. Most of them are less than five centimetres long. They are minnows, and this stretch of river is the minnow reach – one of five major zones found in a typical river. As we look far upstream, we can see the distant hills where the river begins its journey to the sea as a little trickle between moss-covered boulders. This trickle is known as the headstream. Soon it is joined by other trickles, and the increased flow of water carries all the small stones and debris away. The stream now has a rocky bed dotted with large boulders. This stretch is called the troutbeck, for the trout is one of the few fishes that can swim in the fast-moving water. Our minnow reach is below the troutbeck.

Graceful alder trees grow here and there on the banks of the minnow reach. They are easily identified by the small cone-like female catkins. Some are green and still contain developing seeds, but others are hard and woody, with scales gaping to show where the seeds have escaped. In some places the cattle come down for a drink and churn up the ground at the water's edge. Look for the water-starwort growing here – on the mud and in the shallows. It gets its name from the star-shaped clusters of leaves which float at the tips of its stems. Out in the stream, anchored in the gravel, the submerged stems and hair-like leaves of the water-crowfoot trail in the swift current. Minnows are abundant in the water, but trout live here as well. A splash, together with tell-tale circular ripples, tells us that a trout has leapt up to catch an insect flying too close to the water surface. Stickle-backs wriggle in and out of the water-crowfoot, while the

The Water Code

1. Avoid damaging banks and waterside vegetation.
2. Never throw rubbish of any kind on to the banks or into the water.
3. Don't disturb the water where people are fishing.
4. Test the bottom carefully when investigating plantlife or paddling. Keep away from thick mud.
5. Never explore the water-side by yourself.

very spiny miller's thumb or bullhead lurks under the stones. The kingfisher enjoys fishing in the minnow reach. You will probably see no more than a bright blue flash as it skims past, but you might be lucky enough to find its regular perch.

As we follow the narrow riverside path downstream, the surrounding land gradually gets flatter and the river begins to slow down. A tributary joins in and the river widens, but it does not flow any faster. The water is muddy, and lots of mud is deposited along the edges. Bulrushes and many other plants, including great willowherb and yellow iris, are found on these muddy banks. This is the river's lowland reach, also known as the bream reach because the bream is one of the commoner fishes in the murky water. Other fishes include carp, roach, rudd, perch and pike. Swans, coots and moorhens all nest and feed here, and the heron finds much of its food in the shallows.

The lowland reach stretches for a long way, sweeping across the countryside in broad curves. In the far distance lies its final zone – the estuarine reach where the river ends its journey and joins the sea.

Rivers at Work

The enormous amounts of water on the Earth are constantly being circulated. The circulation is known as the water cycle and is powered by the sun. Water evaporates from the surface of the ocean and rises into the air as water vapour. This vapour later condenses and falls as rain or snow. Much of it goes straight back into the sea, but a good deal falls on the land.

Water falling on the very hard and less porous rocks simply runs over the surface and is channelled into small streams. These are the headstreams which are the beginnings of the rivers. Water falling on to softer or more porous rocks, such as chalk or sandstone,

Waterfalls

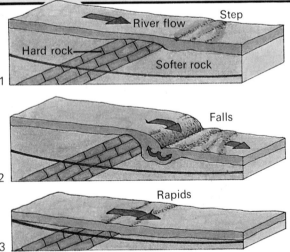

Waterfalls develop when a river runs from a layer of hard rock on to a softer one. The softer rock is worn away more rapidly, leaving the hard one standing up as a step (1). The water rushes over this, and the force of the falling water erodes the softer rock even more quickly. The falls thus get higher and higher (2). But they are not permanent features. The river gradually eliminates them in its struggle to achieve its smooth curve or profile. Slowly it wears away the lip of the falls until eventually they degenerate into rapids, and then disappear altogether (3). The spray thrown up from the waterfall ensures that the surrounding rocks are always wet, and they support a wealth of ferns, mosses, liverworts and other moisture-loving plants (see above). But remember that waterfalls are dangerous places. The rocks are slippery because of the damp vegetation.

Still Waters

From Pond to Dry Land

Ponds and lakes are simply temporary interruptions of the water cycle, holding up water for a while and delaying its return to the sea. Over hundreds, or even millions of years, these areas of fresh water are converted to dry land through the natural processes of succession. It is possible to see marked changes in a pond or a small lake in just a few years. Mud and silt accumulate on the bottom and the pond gradually gets shallower. The reeds and other emergent plants reach out towards the middle as the mud builds up. Dead leaves and other debris collect around the bases of the plants and, before long, the debris rises above the water level in the shallow area around the margin. The swamp plants die out and the marsh plants spread in from the banks. All the open water eventually disappears, being replaced first by swamp and then by marsh. Finally the pond may be converted to dry land.

Above: Lowland ponds like the one pictured here are usually full of nutrients and have plenty of plants growing in them. They are also rich in animal life, with lots of fishes and insects.

soaks into them instead of running over the surface. It generally seeps into the rivers lower down, but it may form its own river by bubbling out of the ground as a spring.

Whatever their origins, the rivers all pour the water back to the sea. But rivers are not just water-carriers. They provide homes for large numbers of plants and animals, and they also play a major role in shaping the land. The water itself can cut a channel by dissolving the rocks – but only very slowly. Much more effective, especially in upland regions, is the action of the vast numbers of stones swept along on the river bed. The stones act like giant ribbons of sandpaper to wear away the river bed and cut the valley deeper and deeper into the hills. In the process, the stones themselves are worn down, and by the time they get to the lower reaches of the river they have been ground down to fine silt and mud.

If the river meets a hollow on its way down to the sea it will turn it into a lake but only until the river can find a way out. The natural processes of succession (see box above) will gradually convert the lake into dry land with the river flowing through it. The river's aim is

to produce a smooth curve or profile from its source to the sea, but millions of years are needed before it achieves this.

Still Waters

Still waters are traditionally divided into lakes and ponds. The larger bodies of water are the lakes, while the smaller ones are generally known as ponds. But there is no fixed size at which a pond becomes a lake. Lakes, however, are generally of natural origin and often very deep. Many have streams running in and out of them, although the bulk of the water remains quite still. Ponds are relatively shallow. Some may be entirely natural, formed when rainwater accumulates in hollows on clay or other non-porous rocks, but most ponds have been made by people. Farm and village ponds, for example, were usually dug out to provide watering places for cattle and horses. No longer needed for this purpose, many ponds are unfortunately disappearing. And with them we are losing the wildlife that lives in and around the water. Naturalists everywhere are trying to save the ponds that are left.

Pond Plant Zones

The surrounding rocks play an important part in determining the types and amounts of wildlife in and around the water. Hard rocks, found mainly in upland regions, release small amounts of minerals to the water. As a result vegetation tends to be sparse around the upland lakes, with just occasional patches of reeds sprouting from the stony shores and a few scattered patches of pondweed on the surface. Even the microscopic floating plants that form the plankton are relatively scarce, and the water is generally very clear. Such lakes are often called *oligotrophic*, which means nutritionally poor. But don't think that they have no animal life at all. Quite a number of caddis flies and stoneflies grow up in these lakes, along with numerous small midges. Their youngsters find enough food in the form of algae and assorted debris on the lake bed, and in turn are eaten by trout and charr – the two main fishes.

Lowland waters tell a very different story. The clays and other relatively soft rocks yield abundant minerals and the waters of both lakes and ponds are very rich. These mineral-rich waters are often called *eutrophic*, which means highly nutritious, and they teem with plant and animal life.

Pond Plant Zones

The plants growing in and around a pond form distinct zones according to the depth of the water. You can investigate this for yourself if you have a suitable pond in your area. Wear wellingtons to wade into the pond but test the firmness of the bottom before each step and don't go on if the bottom is very muddy.

Some pond plants do not actually like to stand in water for very long, and you will find these only on the surrounding banks. They are called marsh plants. Their roots enjoy the damp soil, but the stems remain fairly dry. Common marsh plants which you might find around your pond include marsh marigold, purple loosestrife, great willowherb, common comfrey and water forget-me-not. Right at the water's edge, with water lapping regularly around their bases, grow the swamp plants. These include the yellow iris, bur-

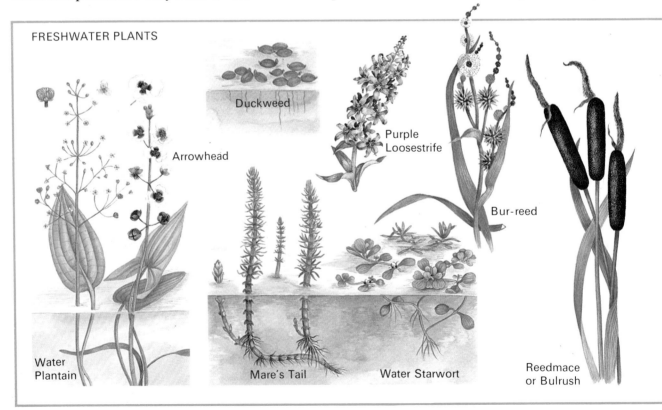

FRESHWATER PLANTS

Duckweed

Arrowhead

Purple Loosestrife

Bur-reed

Water Plantain

Mare's Tail

Water Starwort

Reedmace or Bulrush

Pond Plant Zones

reeds, bulrushes, mare's tail and various large grasses that we call reeds. There are also several sedges, which you can recognize by their triangular stems. Many of these plants extend out to depths of about 15 centimetres and they are commonly called *emergent* plants – because the roots are under the water but the stems and leaves emerge into the air. The arrowhead is a particularly interesting member of this group because it has three very different kinds of leaves. The aerial leaves are shaped just like the heads of arrows and they stand well above the water, but the plant also has oval leaves which float on the surface and very thin, strap-shaped leaves which always remain under the water.

Beyond the reeds and other emergent plants you will probably find many completely submerged species, such as curled pondweed and hornwort. There may also be water lilies and broad-leaved pondweed, both rooted on the bottom but with floating leaves. Scattered among them may be some completely free-floating plants such as frogbit and water soldier. Beware of the latter, for its leaves are edged with very sharp teeth which can cut you very easily. Water lilies sometimes grow in water as much as two metres deep, but generally they prefer shallower water. The free-floating plants, on the other hand, can grow anywhere. But you won't find many at the edge because they would be shaded out by the emergent species.

Light-loving Algae

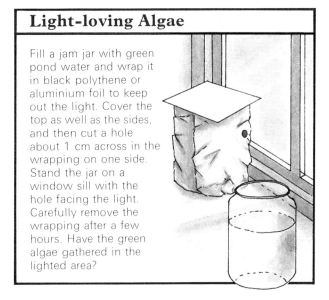

Fill a jam jar with green pond water and wrap it in black polythene or aluminium foil to keep out the light. Cover the top as well as the sides, and then cut a hole about 1 cm across in the wrapping on one side. Stand the jar on a window sill with the hole facing the light. Carefully remove the wrapping after a few hours. Have the green algae gathered in the lighted area?

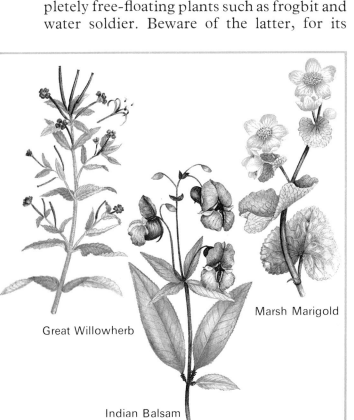

Great Willowherb

Indian Balsam

Marsh Marigold

Investigating Water-weeds

Make a simple drag from three pieces of stout wire bent to form hooks. Attach it to a short stick and tie a long string to the end. Use it for dragging weeds from a pond. Use a stick to measure the depth of water at different distances from the bank and then list the plants occuring at each depth. Watch out for animals crawling among the weeds.

Labelled plastic bags for samples

Jam jars

Drag

Note book

Animals of the Pond

Pond Wildlife

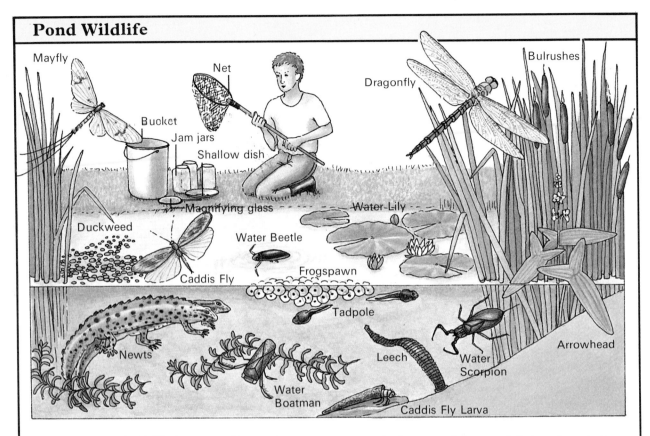

To explore pond wildlife buy a small aquarium net from a pet shop or make one from a length of strong wire and a piece of muslin or the foot of an old nylon stocking. Bend the wire into a circle roughly 15 centimetres across and sew the net bag to it. You can then fix your net to a handle about one metre long. It is a good idea to flatten one side of the net frame, for this makes it easier to push the net across the bottom of the pond. Take a few shallow dishes and a hand lens or magnifying glass to examine creatures on the spot. Dishes with white bottoms are best, although clear glass will be fine if you stand them on white paper. A bucket and jam jars are useful for holding samples. Don't forget to return all the animals and plants to the pond when you have finished looking at them.

Tiny duckweeds float on nearly all ponds and are sometimes so numerous that they completely cover the surface with a brilliant green carpet. Take a spoonful of these little plants and float them in a jar of water. See how each plant consists of just a flattened disc, known as a *thallus*. Notice the thread-like roots hanging down into the water. During the spring and summer each thallus produces a succession of buds, which eventually break off and form new plants. Within days, these new plants are producing buds themselves, and this is how the duckweed spreads so rapidly over a pond. The plants also produce flowers and seeds at certain times. The flowers have no petals and they are too small to be seen without a powerful magnifying glass. They develop in tiny pouches at the edge of the thallus.

The duckweeds are among the smallest of all flowering plants, but they are by no means the smallest plants in the pond. This honour goes to the microscopic algae that swim in the water by waving their whip-like hairs. There are often so many of them that the water turns green in the summer. These minute plants provide food for many tiny animals, and also for some larger ones like the freshwater mussels. The latter simply draw in currents of water and filter out the algae.

Caddis Fly Cases

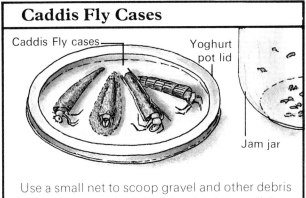

Caddis Fly cases

Yoghurt pot lid

Jam jar

Use a small net to scoop gravel and other debris from the stream bed. Put the debris in a dish or lid and search for caddis cases like those shown above. See how the small stones or bits of leaf are neatly stuck together to form the case. Each species has its own design.

Animals of the Pond

Even a small pond contains hundreds of different kinds of animals. There are plant-eaters and predators, and each kind occupies its own particular niche in the pond environment. Many of the animals can be seen properly only with the aid of a microscope, but they exist in immense numbers and play a vital role in feeding the larger animals.

The best way to collect and study pond dwellers is to use a small net and a number of shallow dishes. But before you start churning up the water with your net, take a few minutes to look at the whole pond environment. Look out for dragonflies flashing through the air with wings rustling as they hunt for flies. Swallows and martins may also swoop low over the water to snatch up the flies, and the grey wagtail often flits nimbly around the water's edge to capture insects. Have a good look, too, at the water surface, for several insects actually live and feed here. As they skate about and capture other insects that fall on to the pond, they are kept up by surface tension – a sort of elastic skin on the surface of the water. The pond skaters are the best-known of these surface-dwellers, but they are shy insects and will skid rapidly for cover if alarmed. Approach very carefully if you want to watch them, and then you might be able to pick out the little dimple that each

foot makes in the water surface. Keep an eye open for the whirligig beetles as well – shiny black beetles that skim round and round on the surface like tiny clockwork toys. You will also see other beetles, together with pond snails and water bugs, rising to the surface every now and then to renew their air supplies. These creatures are rather like scuba-divers, taking their air supplies down with them in containers of various kinds. The snails have lung-like cavities inside their bodies, while water beetles carry their air in the space between the body and the tough wing cases.

When you start to explore below the surface, sweep your net gently to and fro through the water and empty it into a dish of

From Tadpole to Frog

Collect a small amount of frogspawn from a pond and put it in an aquarium with pond water and plenty of water plants. Watch how the eggs gradually change shape as the tadpoles develop. How long do they take to hatch? Watch the baby tadpoles feed on the plants at first. Later they will need animal food. Give them *small* pieces of meat—attached to cotton so that you can pull the remains of the meat out easily before it goes bad. Release the tadpoles back into the pond as soon as all four legs have appeared, for it is very difficult to feed the young frogs at this stage.

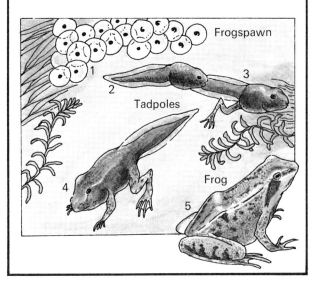

Frogspawn

Tadpoles

Frog

In the Water-weeds

pond water after every couple of sweeps. Take samples from near the surface, from midwater, and from the bottom, and check the kinds of animals in each one. You probably won't find much difference in the first two samples, but the bottom sample will contain many crawling animals that are absent from the other two samples. Don't be surprised to see clusters of leaf fragments or small twigs moving across the bottom of your dish. Look closely and you will see an insect grub poking out from the front of each cluster. The grub is a young caddis fly and it uses the twig or leaf fragments to make a portable house: the fragments are stuck to a tube of silk which the grub spins from its own body. Mayfly nymphs, easily recognized by their three slender 'tails', crawl over or burrow in the mud as a rule, but some swim quite actively. Dragonfly nymphs are fierce predators, shooting out their spiny jaws to catch other animals: they will even attack small fishes. The great diving beetle is another powerful predator.

Newts can be found in the ponds mainly in the spring, when the males are dressed in bright courtship colours and sport frilly crests on their backs and tails. Watch how the males dance around the plumper and less showy females and quiver their tails. Later you might see the females laying their eggs: each one is laid singly and carefully wrapped in a leaf. Newts are amphibians, like the frogs and toads, and the youngsters spend several months in the water as tadpoles.

Small ponds do not usually contain many fish species, although there may be large numbers of individuals. Fishes obtain their oxygen direct from the water by means of their gills and they do not come to the surface for air. Most of them are rather active animals and they need plenty of oxygen, especially when there is a lot of rotting vegetation. The few fishes that can tolerate pond conditions include sticklebacks, perch and carp. The last two species often remain very small through overcrowding. Larger lakes, with plenty of open water, produce much bigger fishes and also support many more species.

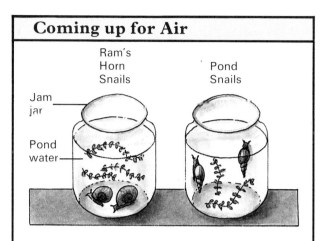

Coming up for Air

Jam jar / Pond water / Ram's Horn Snails / Pond Snails

Collect two or three great pond snails and the same number of ram's horn snails. Put them in separate jam jars of pond water and watch them carefully for half an hour. How many visits do the snails make to the surface to renew their air supplies? Just count the total visits without noting the individual snails. You will find that the ram's horns do not come up much at all. Their bodies contain haemoglobin — the red pigment that occurs in our blood — and this helps them to absorb oxygen direct from the water. Pond snails have no haemoglobin and cannot absorb much oxygen from the water: they have to surface frequently for air.

Examine the Water-weeds

Many pond and lake animals spend their lives crawling among the water-weeds. You might dislodge some with your net, but a better way of collecting these animals is to drag out a few weeds and examine them in a dish. Look for water beetles and mayfly nymphs attached to the weeds, and notice the large claws which give them a secure grip. Small leeches may stretch and contract as they loop their way over the vegetation. Sausage-shaped blobs of jelly are the egg masses of water snails. Look also for the fascinating *Hydra*, a tiny freshwater relative of the sea anemones. Only a few millimetres long, it attaches itself mainly to the underside of leaves and its slender tentacles dangle in the water to catch water fleas or other small animals that bump into them. The victims are held fast by the hydra's stinging harpoons.

Fishing for Worms

The pond is full of scavenging creatures, which you can catch quite easily by tying a piece of meat to a length of string and hanging it in the water. Pull it out after about 15 minutes and examine it. The most common animals will be small dark flatworms. Put them into a dish of pond water to watch them at work.

Little black or brown animals glide smoothly over the water plants like pieces of ribbon. These are flatworms and they feed on a wide range of living and dead matter. You can also find them on the bottom of the pond, and they even glide upside-down beneath the water surface. A good way to collect these creatures is to hang a piece of meat in the pond for a while (see left). Flatworms have amazing powers of survival and recovery. They can survive without food for months, although they get smaller and smaller during this time, and if you cut them in half each piece will quickly grow into a new animal. In fact, you can cut them into dozens of pieces and each piece will grow. What is more, each piece 'remembers' which was the front and always grows its new head at the right end.

Life in the River

As we have already seen, a river varies a great deal from place to place along its course. Each stretch, or reach, has its own assortment of wildlife. The lowland reach, where the water moves quite slowly, is very similar to the lowland lake or pond, although there are more kinds of fish in the river. Bream, tench, perch, roach, rudd and pike all occur regularly in the

Set up an Aquarium

You can keep many pond creatures at home in a simple glass or plastic aquarium. Put some clean sand or gravel and a few stones on the bottom of the tank (not a fish bowl), together with a few plants. Stand the tank in the light, but not in the full sun and fill it with pond water. Sticklebacks do well in a simple aquarium, and you can add most of the common pond creatures as well, but avoid dragonfly nymphs and the great diving beetle: these will eat the other animals. Add water fleas from time to time to feed the fishes.

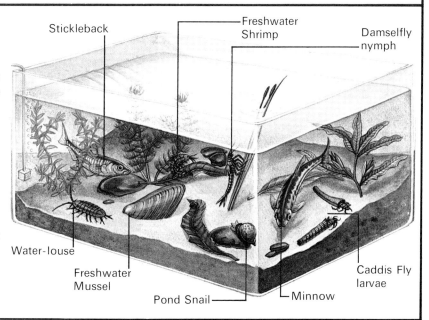

Stickleback

Freshwater Shrimp

Damselfly nymph

Water-louse

Freshwater Mussel

Pond Snail

Minnow

Caddis Fly larvae

Freshwater Fishes

lowland river, and there are often many eels as well. Canals are also very similar to lakes and lowland rivers. All these waters have rather muddy bottoms, with plenty of water weeds and many emergent plants along the edges.

Further upstream, however, in the minnow reach and the troutbeck, the conditions are very different. The swift currents of the troutbeck scour the river bed and carry away all the small stones and mud. Few plants can establish themselves at the water's edge, and none at all grow in the middle. Only strong swimmers can maintain themselves in the open water, and the trout is obviously the main fish living here. Loach and miller's thumb stay close to the bottom, where the current is a little slower, and minnows sometimes manage to live in some of the quieter pools along the margins. Try measuring the speed of the current by throwing a twig into the middle and timing it over 50 or 100 metres.

There is plenty of insect life on the bottom of the stream, feeding mainly on plant debris carried down by the current. The mayfly nymphs living here are very flat, quite unlike the burrowing forms living in lakes and ponds, and they cling tightly to the stones so that they are not dislodged by the current. Stonefly nymphs are also found here. They resemble mayfly nymphs in many ways, but have only two 'tails'. Look for the fragile empty skins on the waterside stones, showing where the nymphs have crawled out of the water, split their skins and pulled themselves out as adult insects.

Many caddis flies breed in the swift currents of the troutbeck and minnow reach, but instead of using plant fragments to make their cases the larvae use small stones. The stones weigh the insects down and prevent them from being washed away. The larva of *Anabolia* always attaches some small sticks to its case: these probably protect the larvae from the trout, which gobble up most kinds of caddis grubs, but they also have another function. Search for some occupied cases on the stream bed. Notice how they all lie with the head end facing upstream. The twigs help to line them up in this way, and then debris drifting along the stream bed is brought right to the larval mouths. A few caddis grubs

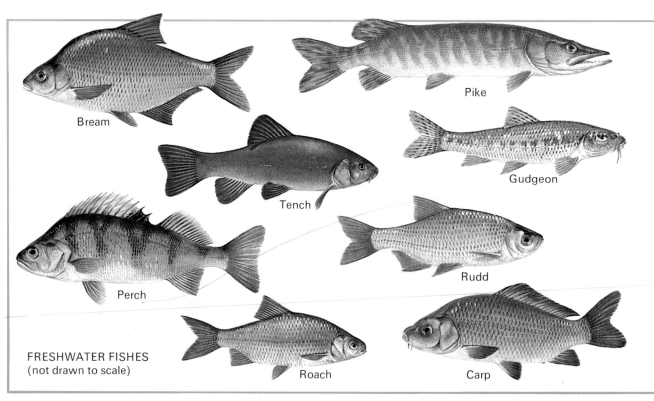

Bream

Pike

Tench

Gudgeon

Perch

Rudd

FRESHWATER FISHES
(not drawn to scale)

Roach

Carp

The Aggressive Stickleback

Capture a male stickleback in the spring at the beginning of the breeding season. You can easily distinguish the males by the red throat and belly. Put your fish in a small aquarium with some gravel and plenty of water plants. He defends his territory very vigorously and, in nature, drives away any other male stickleback. Put a small mirror in the aquarium and watch the fish attack his own reflection in the belief that it is another male.

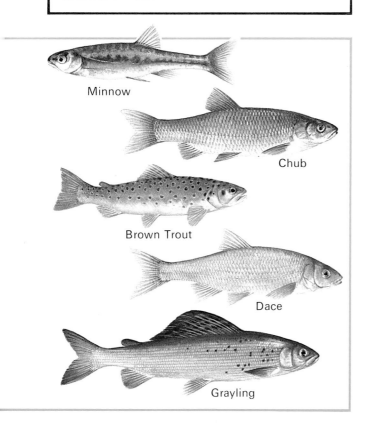

Minnow

Chub

Brown Trout

Dace

Grayling

cement their cases permanently to large stones on the river bed.

The current is a little slower in the minnow reach which is also known as the grayling reach on the continent because there the grayling is especially common in this zone. Banks of gravel build up here and there, especially on the insides of bends, and various plants are able to establish themselves. The current flows faster around the outsides of the bends, eroding the banks more quickly and cutting deeper channels. This is where you should look for the fishes. Gudgeon and chub live here as well as the minnows and grayling. Trout spawn on the beds of gravel, and salmon also spawn in this zone in some rivers. Here, too, the colourful male stickleback makes his tunnel-shaped nest by gluing bits of weed together with secretion from his body. He then attracts a female with an intricate courtship dance and leads her to his nest. After she has laid her eggs, the male looks after them and the babies when they hatch.

Dace, roach and rudd begin to appear as you move down towards the lowland reach. Keep your eyes open for the crayfish which looks like a small brown lobster. It lurks under stones by day and comes out to catch other animals at night.

Waterside Bird-watching

The banks of both still and moving waters are excellent habitats for birds. Look for the beautiful kingfisher all the way along the river from the troutbeck down. As long as it has a suitable perch from which to watch the water it will be able to dive in and catch small fishes. But this bird also needs a good bank somewhere in which to dig its nest burrow. You are most likely to see the dipper on the upper parts of the river, perching on boulders and bobbing up and down on midstream stones. Then it disappears by simply walking into the water. Under the surface it can walk or swim while searching for caddis grubs and other insects. The heron prefers to fish in quieter waters with plenty of vegetation around the edges. Look for it in the lowland

Identifying Birds

WATERSIDE BIRDS

Moorhen

Grey Wagtail

Reed Warbler

summer

winter

Little Egret

winter

Dabchick

summer

Dipper

Kingfisher

Coot

female

male

Marsh Harrier

female

male

Reed Bunting

reach of the river and also around canals and lakes. It catches frogs and other animals as well as fishes.

It is a good idea to build a simple hide close to a pond or a lake, or a slow-moving river, for many birds live here and stay in more or less one place for long periods. Make it with a frame of branches covered with an old sheet dyed green and a few leafy twigs, and be prepared to sit in it quietly for long periods. From your hide you will be able to watch swans, ducks, coots, moorhens and grebes, among other interesting birds. Some of the birds are illustrated above. Many of them nest among the waterside vegetation, or even on rafts of dead plants. Watch the ducks feeding. There are two main groups. The mallard belongs to the group known as dabbling ducks: they feed by putting their heads into the water or by up-ending themselves and

Above: A female mallard takes her brood of ducklings for a swim. The ducklings are able to swim almost as soon as they hatch from the eggs.

winter

summer

Red-throated Diver

Great Crested Grebe

Grey Heron

female

male

Goosander

Binoculars by the Water

Ducks and other water birds often swim far out on lakes or on the sea, so you will need binoculars to identify them and to study them properly. Choose a fairly powerful pair if you are likely to do most of your bird-watching by the water. A practical size is 9×40 which magnifies 9 times but is still not too heavy. Another good size is 8×40, but if you can afford a light-weight pair choose 10×24 or 10×30. These will give you a better magnification with less weight, but they are not so useful at dusk because the small objective lenses, only 24 or 30 millimetres across, do not let much light through. Keep your binoculars strapped around your neck at all times so that they can't fall into the water. Practise following birds in flight with your binoculars but be very careful not to point them at the sun as this could blind you.

leaving just the tail sticking out of the water. The other group are known as diving ducks. They feed by diving right under the surface. The tufted duck is a typical diving duck. Watch to find out what sort of things both groups of duck eat – apart from the bread that people like to give them.

Winter is a very good time for watching ducks in Britain and other parts of western Europe, for huge numbers fly in from the north when their ponds and lakes start to freeze over. Many geese and swans come too.

Under the Ice

Have you ever wondered what happens to fishes and other aquatic animals when their ponds freeze over in the winter? In fact, the ice forms an insulating blanket for the lower layers, and the water at the bottom usually remains well above freezing point. Life can carry on almost as normal, although everything slows down as the temperature falls. Fishes become very lethargic and spend most of their time sitting quietly on the bottom. Many other creatures do the same, but some of the smaller animals go into a true resting stage, surrounded by a thick coat which can resist very low temperatures. Because they move very little, the animals require little oxygen: there is usually enough dissolved in the water to keep them going, and as long as the ice is not too thick or covered with snow the submerged plants can continue to make food by photosynthesis, with the consequent release of more oxygen.

Plants which float at or near the surface in summer often sink to the bottom in winter. The duckweed stores a lot of starch in the autumn and its thalli become swollen and heavy. They sink to the bottom of the pond, but by the end of the winter they have used up much of the stored food and they are light enough to float up again and resume normal life. In very cold winters the ice may exceed 15 centimetres in depth, but it rarely exceeds 25 centimetres in Britain. So if your garden pond is at least 50 centimetres deep in the centre, there will always be some free water for your fishes.

Fossils

Collect Fossils

Next time you visit seaside cliffs, take a close look to see if you can find any fossils in the rocks. Fossils are the remains of animals and plants that lived and died long ago when the rocks themselves were being formed. But not all cliffs contain fossils: granite cliffs have no fossils because the granite was formed from molten rock deep in the Earth. Limestones, on the other hand, are often very rich in fossils. These rocks were formed in shallow water and they contain the shells and other remains of huge numbers of sea creatures. Some limestones are made almost entirely of fossils. In some places you can see huge banks of shells piled up on the beach. In time, these may be covered with sand or mud and converted to fossils.

Don't be tempted to climb up the rocks in search of fossils, for cliffs can be very dangerous. You can often find fossils at the base of the cliffs, especially where the rocks are relatively soft. The fossils tend to be harder than the surrounding rock and they fall out as the rock gradually crumbles away. You might see some standing out from the face of the rock, and then you can chip them out quite easily. You could also make sketches of the fossils and note down their measurements in your notebook. This will help you to identify them later.

Studying Your Finds

Carry your fossils home wrapped in newspaper, but stick a label on them first so that you know exactly where you found them. You can clean the fossils up at home with an old toothbrush. Try to find out what kinds of animal or plant produced your fossils, and also try to find out how old they are. Your local library or school may have a geological map which will tell you the approximate age of the rocks in your area. Some rocks are hundreds of millions of years old, and so are the fossils that you find in them (see page 8). Try to discover how your fossils were formed. Some are shells that have literally been turned to stone in the rocks, but many fossils are simply hollow moulds left behind when a shell or other object has been dissolved away. The pattern of the shell is then left in the rock, just as you can produce a pattern by pressing a shell into a piece of clay.

Sea cliffs are not the only places where you can find fossils. Look for them wherever rocks are exposed – in the mountains, in quarries, and even by roadworks. The clay and other rocks dug out from the trenches often contain lots of fossils.

A few of the more common kinds of fossil are illustrated here, but don't expect to find them all in one area. They come from rocks of very different ages.

Below: Here are some examples of the sort of fossils you might find at the base of cliffs.

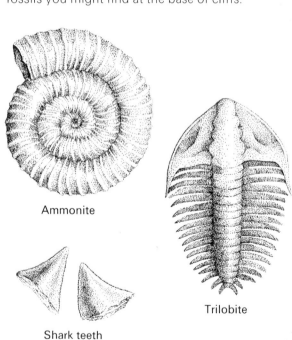

Ammonite

Shark teeth

Trilobite

Belemnite

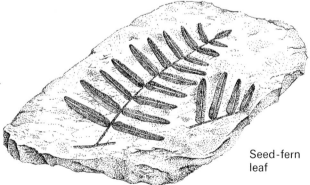

Seed-fern leaf

MOUNTAINS AND MOORLANDS

Mountains tower above the rest of the Earth's surface but the rocks they are made of often contain the remains of sea creatures, which prove that the mountains were once beneath the sea. Although mountain tops are always cold and windy places, many plants and animals manage to survive in the harsh climate.

Explore the unusual wildlife of these wild and desolate habitats. Discover how moorlands were created by people and their grazing animals. Find out how mountain animals keep themselves warm and how insects avoid being blown away by the strong winds. See how the vegetation changes as you climb a mountain and learn to recognize some of the beautiful mountain flowers.

Mountains and Moorlands

How high does a hill have to be before it can be called a mountain? There is no simple answer to this question. In Britain, hills more than about 600 metres high are generally regarded as mountains, but British mountains are very tiny compared with those in other parts of the world. Scotland's Ben Nevis is our highest peak, but at a mere 1347 metres it is little more than a quarter the height of Mont Blanc, which is the highest peak in the Alps. And Mont Blanc is not much more than half the height of Everest, which towers up to 8848 metres in the Himalayas. A peak of 600 metres in the Himalayas would be regarded as a very small hill indeed.

Mountains can be dangerous places and it is difficult to explore the wilder parts without special training and equipment. Many roads go through the Alps, however, and if you are lucky enough to visit this region you will be able to see quite a lot of mountain plants and animals without too much effort. The lower slopes are clothed with farmland or with deciduous woodland, but as you get higher you will see that pines and firs and other coniferous trees gradually take over. Higher still, the trees start to thin out and you will see the lush alpine meadows. The highest level at which trees can grow is called the *tree line*. You can see the line very clearly on some mountains, but it is not always at the same level. It is at about 1800 metres on the south-facing slopes of the Alps, but on the cooler, north-facing slopes it is about 300 metres lower. On the mountains of Scotland and Scandinavia the tree line is lower still.

It is above the tree line that the real mountain life is to be found. You will see scattered shrubs, many of them lying almost flat on the ground

The Tree Line

High up on a mountainside it is too cold and windy for trees to grow. This level is known as the *tree line* and it is clearly visible on the photograph below. Trees can grow up to a higher level on warmer, south-facing slopes than on colder, north-facing slopes. The tree line is also higher up on warmer mountains in the south than it is on colder, northern mountains.

where they avoid the worst of the wind, but the main vegetation is short grass – studded with thousands of beautiful flowers in the summer. As you go even higher, the soil gets thinner and the shrubs disappear. Even the grass thins out after a while and you will find yourself surrounded by bare, shattered rock with just a few tufts of grass and other hardy plants. Examine some of the shattered rock. You might find fossils of sea creatures, showing that the rocks, which might now be 2500 metres above sea level, were once beneath the sea. Mountains have been pushed up by immense forces inside the Earth.

Notice how cold and windy it is on the higher parts of the mountain. For every 200 metres that you climb, the temperature drops by just over 1°C. On the top of the highest peaks you will find snow even in the middle of summer. The plants and animals that live on these slopes have many special features that help them to cope with the cold.

The cold is largely responsible for shattering the rocks on the mountain tops. Water collects in small cracks and, when it freezes, the ice opens the cracks even further, gradually splitting the rocks into smaller pieces. Each spring, the melting snows carry some of the stones further down the mountain, starting them on their long journey back to the sea by way of the mountain streams and the rivers. So the mountains are not permanent features of the Earth's surface. They are continually being worn down and will eventually disappear, although it takes many millions of years to wear down a large mountain.

Mountain Flowers

Flowers in the Mountains

As the trees thin out towards the tree line, patches of grassland take their place. These are the famous alpine meadows and in early summer they are full of beautiful flowers, which flourish on the mountain slopes because of the rich soil and abundant moisture provided by the melting snows. At lower levels the trees may be cleared to make way for artificial meadows. These are soon colonized by the abundant wild flowers, which provide nutritious hay for feeding the cattle in winter. The flowers on these slopes include many kinds of orchid, columbine, and lily – including the stately martagon lily. Some flowers, like the martagon lily, are protected by law because they are becoming rare. Leave the flowers for other people to enjoy. Then they will scatter their seeds and produce more flowers in the future.

You must go even higher to find the true alpine flowers – the ones people love to grow in rock gardens at home. There are some dwarf shrubs in this zone, including the juniper and the lovely alpenrose. They all sprawl over the ground and are rarely more than a few centimetres high. Shoots that dare to poke up any higher are quickly killed by the cold winds. But the shrubs can grow a little larger in the shelter of boulders, where there is protection from the wind and a regular supply of water. The thin soils of the upper slopes dry out very quickly in the summer, but moisture remains under the boulders.

Mountain Survival

Famous alpine plants include the brilliant blue gentians, pinks and primulas of many kinds, saxifrages, crocuses, and the fur-coated edelweiss. Nearly all these grow in dense mats or cushions, hugging the ground to escape the worst of the wind and get as

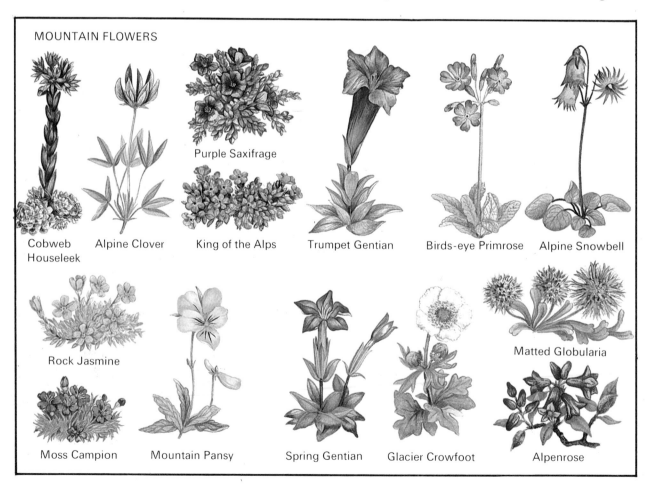

MOUNTAIN FLOWERS

Cobweb Houseleek   Alpine Clover   Purple Saxifrage   King of the Alps   Trumpet Gentian   Birds-eye Primrose   Alpine Snowbell

Rock Jasmine   Moss Campion   Mountain Pansy   Spring Gentian   Glacier Crowfoot   Matted Globularia   Alpenrose

much heat as possible from the ground itself. The dense growth also helps to trap warmth and moisture around the short stems and leaves. Coatings of hair have the same function and you will find them on many alpine plants. The edelweiss has extremely furry flower-heads, but the best known hairy plant is perhaps the cobweb houseleek. Commonly grown as a pot plant, this species covers its globular leaf rosettes with strands of fine hair looking just like cobwebs. Like many other alpines, it has rather juicy leaves, which store water to see it through the summer on the thin, stony soil. Moisture is essential for strong growth, and all the alpines do best if they can get their roots under the large stones or into deep cracks in the rocks where there is permanent moisture.

The alpines are covered by snow for at least half of the year and they have a very short growing season. The mats or cushions grow very little from year to year, but the growth of the flowers themselves is usually very rapid. They generally open as soon as the snow has melted and scatter their seeds within a few weeks. Some – such as crocuses and snowbells – flower even before the surrounding snow has melted. The leaves then start building up their food stores ready for the next year. Those leaves that have no fur coats are often very dark in colour. This is because dark colours absorb heat more efficiently than pale ones. You will notice that the flowers of many alpines are also rather dark.

There are few annual plants in the alpine zone. The short growing season allows only the fastest-growing species to grow from seed and scatter more seeds in the same year. If spring is late or the autumn snows come early, the whole population of these short-lived plants can be wiped out. Even the perennial plants often have back-up systems which ensure that they can reproduce themselves if the flowers and seeds fail. Many produce small detachable buds that take root when they fall to the ground. If you look at some of the mountain grasses you might see some of these little buds sprouting on the flower-heads even before they fall.

Insects in the Mountains

If you reach the edge of the snow line, you will be amazed at the number of insects you can see there. Most of them are tiny springtails (see page 31), which are often so numerous they turn the snow black. The sparse vegetation of the upper slopes supports a few hardy grasshoppers and earwigs, together with various bugs. Most of these insects are flightless and many are wingless as well. Flight would be of little use to these small insects because they would almost certainly be swept away if they took off in the strong winds. Look out for spiders sunbathing on stones and low-growing plants. Most of them are wolf spiders. They make no webs and simply chase after their flightless prey. Mountain spiders and insects tend to be darker than their lowland relatives.

When the alpine flowers come out you will see furry bumble bees and butterflies feeding on pollen and nectar. Notice that they stay close to the ground to avoid being blown away. Brown butterflies with eye-spots around the edges are particularly common. There are about 50 different kinds in the Alps, all very similar but each with a slightly different pattern. Many of these butterflies have very restricted ranges.

Golden eagles build huge nests of sticks on remote rock ledges. This adult is tearing up food for its chick, which is about three weeks old and still covered with down.

Mountain Animals

Mountain Birds

You will see few small birds on the upper slopes; the winds are far too strong for most of them. But you may catch a glimpse of the fluttering pink wings of the wallcreeper as it flits about a rock face searching for insects.

Larger birds are more at home in the mountains; they can soar and glide quite easily on the strong winds. The long, narrow, scythe-like wings of the alpine swift and the aerobatic skills of the raven and alpine chough enable these birds to thrive among the high peaks. But it is the birds of prey that most often spring to mind when we think of mountain birds. The majestic golden eagle is occasionally to be seen gliding to and fro, scouring the slopes for hares and marmots. Rarer still is the handsome lammergeyer, also known as the bearded vulture. Dead animals provide most of its food. Although the mountain animals are generally very sure-footed, accidents do occur and vultures are quick to take advantage of them. The lammergeyer can even deal with the bones, often carrying them aloft and dropping them on to the rocks so they shatter and expose the marrow.

Mammals

A fair number of fur-coated animals manage to survive on the sparse vegetation of the upper slopes. The one that you are most likely

An alpine marmot must always be alert to eagles and other dangers and is always ready to dash back to its burrow in the mountainside.

Mountain Butterflies

The apollo, seen here feeding at a thistle, is one of the most beautiful of the alpine butterflies. With a furry coat to keep it warm, it floats lazily over the meadows and grassy slopes up to a height of about 1800m. Its plump, black caterpillar eats the fleshy leaves of stonecrop plants. The apollo is protected by law in many European countries.

to see in the Alps is the alpine marmot, a bundle of fur that tumbles down the slopes at high speed when alarmed. About 60 centimetres long, it lives in a deep, grass-lined burrow above the tree line. The marmots sleep through the winter, whereas the mountain hare merely moves further down the slope and turns white for added protection. The ibex and the chamois are the largest of the mountain grazers. The ibex lives above the tree line all year round. In winter it has to scrape away the snow with its hooves before it can reach the vegetation, although in the most exposed places the wind may actually keep the slopes free of snow. The ibex can climb the steepest slopes with the aid of its specialized hooves; the large dew-claw at the back provides a secure grip. The chamois has similar dew-claws and it also has suction cups on its hooves which make it a very sure-footed climber. It can make astonishing leaps and has shock absorbers in its feet to ensure that it makes a soft landing. The chamois moves down into the forest for winter.

The Bleak Moorland

Moorland Vegetation

Only the highest British mountains reach above the tree line, but even on the lower slopes trees are scarce. On upland areas in Britain the commonest vegetation is moorland. Although the moors are ancient they are not natural. They were formed during the Bronze Age and Iron Age, between 4000 and 2000 years ago, when huge areas of forest were cut down to make way for farming.

Heavy rainfall has also played a part in the formation of moorlands. The soils tend to become waterlogged and thick beds of peat develop. Decay is very slow in the cold, wet climate and the plant remains – largely *Sphagnum* or bog-moss – can reach depths of several metres. Huge areas of upland are clothed with this peat; they are known as blanket bogs. It is sometimes possible to see the remains of ancient tree stumps where the peat blanket has been worn away – proof that the area was once covered with trees. The seedlings cannot establish themselves on the acidic peat today, however, and the moors are

A male red grouse surveys his moorland territory. The red grouse, which is found only in Britain and Ireland, feeds on heather. Many moors are deliberately burnt from time to time to encourage fresh new growth for this important game bird.

left to shrubs such as heather and bilberry, together with various tough grasses and other low-growing plants. Relatively few plant species can cope with the acidity and the shortage of minerals. Most of the useful plant foods are unobtainable, locked up in the undecayed plant remains in the peat.

Cotton-grass is common on the moister parts of the moors and turns them white with its fluffy fruiting heads in the summer. In wetter areas you may also find the insect-eating sundew. This fascinating plant has sticky tentacles on its leaves, which are death traps for the hordes of tiny midges that breed in the waterlogged peat. When an insect lands on a leaf, the tentacles gradually fold over the insect and then the whole leaf closes around it and starts to digest it. This is how the sundew compensates for the shortage of minerals in the peat.

Moorland Management

Some moorlands are now being replanted with forests after a certain amount of ploughing and drainage. Other areas are maintained for rearing grouse, which feed on young heather shoots. Landowners periodically burn off the old heather branches to encourage new shoots to spring up. These fires prevent any possible regrowth by trees.

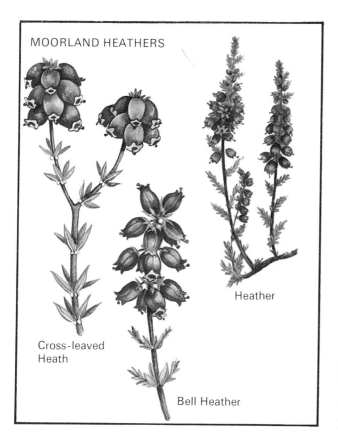

MOORLAND HEATHERS

Cross-leaved Heath

Bell Heather

Heather

The Lowland Heath

Heathland Plants

Forest clearance on sandy or gravelly soils in the lowlands has led to the formation of the heathlands. These resemble the moors in being covered largely by heather and related plants, but they are much drier and there is little or no peat. The soils are rather poor because the rainwater washes the minerals down through the sand to much lower levels.

Despite the poor soils, the heathlands support a greater variety of plants than the moors. As well as the heathers, you will find gorse and broom. All of these shrubs are able to increase their mineral supplies with the aid of fungi or bacteria in their roots. You will also find many lichens, together with flowers such as harebell and tormentil. Look out for the dodder, a strange parasitic plant that looks like strands of red cotton smothering the heather and gorse. It has no roots or leaves and steals all its food by sending suckers into other plants.

Pine and birch trees can easily invade the heathland, and have done in many areas, but the dry heathland often catches fire in summer and this prevents the trees from becoming established.

Butterflies and Moths

Heathland butterflies include the grayling and the silver-studded blue. You may also see the emperor moth (see pages 60, 62) at the end of April and in May. Look for its large green and black caterpillars on the heather in June.

The Soil of the Heath

Just below the plant debris is a pale band of sand from which almost all the minerals have been removed by the water draining through the soil. Lower down, the sand becomes browner again where the minerals are re-deposited.

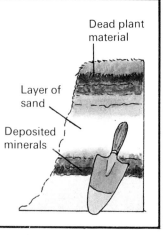

Dead plant material

Layer of sand

Deposited minerals

Lowland heaths are often very dry and frequently catch fire. This prevents trees from swamping the heathland, but does not permanently harm the vegetation. Fire can actually benefit the plants by burning off the old stems and allowing fresh ones to spring from the roots. The roots are not usually harmed when the fire sweeps across the surface. Here you can see fresh shoots of birch and bell heather springing up on burnt ground, together with carpets of hair moss. Birds and insects also benefit from the fresh young shoots.

PARKS AND GARDENS

Parks and gardens are very important miniature nature reserves, although they are artificial habitats. Even in the middle of the towns, these habitats can attract and support a variety of wildlife, especially birds and insects.

Explore the area around your home and discover some of the many plants and animals that have taken up residence there. Learn to identify garden birds and find out which plants will encourage butterflies to visit your garden. Learn how to make a pond for frogs and newts and unearth the importance of the humble earthworm.

Parks and Gardens

Our parks and gardens are entirely artificial, but you can still learn a great deal about natural history by studying the plant and animal life in them. Take a good look at the illustration on the right and you will see just how rich in wildlife a park or garden can become. Look at the wide range of habitats that have been created: lawns, paths, walls and fences, shrubberies and trees, ponds, flower beds and vegetable plots. Most of these have their natural equivalents in the wild and it is not surprising that wild plants and animals quickly move in.

Park and garden walls, for instance, are similar to rocky hillsides and coastal cliffs as a habitat. The old walls in the park in the picture are covered with wild plants, such as wallflowers, which grow wild on cliffs. Several birds also make their homes on walls, like the house martin here which tucks its nest under the eaves of the house. House martins still nest on cliffs and rocky places in the wild, but far more of them now nest on buildings. They may be even more common now than they were in earlier times when there were fewer houses. The same is true of the swallow which used to nest mainly in caves but now nests almost entirely in buildings. It likes more cover than the house martin and its favourite nesting sites are buildings with fairly wide entrances, such as barns, covered markets and railway stations. House sparrows and pigeons will nest on buildings even in the busiest parts of town.

Only in parks and gardens can you find so many different habitats in such small areas – perhaps only a few square metres in a town garden. Each habitat has its own assortment of wildlife. Count the different kinds of animals you can find in the illustration here. You'll catch sight of many of them in your own garden or local park, although you are unlikely to find them all at one time. Parks and gardens are obviously very important havens for wildlife, and they could become even more important in the future as more and more of the countryside is built on.

Investigating the Habitats

In the following pages we will explore all these different habitats. All you will need in the way of equipment is a notebook in which to record your observations. A hand lens for close examinations and binoculars for watching birds and other animals from a distance (see page 144) will also be useful. There are plenty of ways in which you can make your own garden especially attractive to wildlife. Butterflies and other insects, for example, will appreciate lots of nectar-filled flowers, while many birds enjoy berry-bearing shrubs in the autumn. You can also provide extra food for the birds in the winter and encourage them to nest in the garden by putting up nesting boxes. Make your garden as varied as possible and you will always have plenty of wildlife to watch.

Garden Birds

The Birds in Your Garden

The birds pictured on this page are some of the many kinds that you might see in your garden. Some of them may actually nest in the trees and shrubs, or even on your house, while others merely come for food. You can increase the number and variety of visitors by putting out food in the autumn and winter. It is well worth buying a seed mixture specially chosen for wild birds. These mixtures contain seeds of many sizes and please a wide variety of birds. Crush some of the seeds with a rolling pin before putting them out: this will make them more attractive to robins and other slender-billed birds. Peanuts – not salted – threaded on strings or put into little net bags are thoroughly enjoyed by the tits and greenfinches.

Most kinds of table scraps are accepted by the birds. You can put them on the bird table just as they are, but it is more fun to mix them into a bird pudding. Pour melted dripping or other fat over the scraps in a basin and leave the mixture to set. Then turn it out on the bird table and watch the birds queuing up to feed. Mix some oatmeal and dried fruit with the scraps to make the pudding even more nourishing.

Feeding Birds

The traditional bird table will attract lots of birds to your garden, A baffle will prevent rats and squirrels from climbing and stealing the food and hurting the birds. Try hanging up a fresh coconut for blue tits and great tits. Fill the shell with bird pudding when the coconut has gone. Put bird pudding and peanuts into holes drilled in a small log. Tits and woodpeckers will enjoy this. Don't forget water for bathing and drinking.

Table
Coconut
Small log
Water
Baffle

SOME GARDEN BIRDS

Redstart
male
female

female
male
Black Redstart (rare in Britain)

Collared Dove

Hoopoe (rare in Britain)

Cuckoo

Wren

Jackdaw

You don't have to be good at woodwork to make a bird table. A piece of wood about 30 centimetres long and 20 centimetres wide nailed to the top of a sturdy post makes a perfectly good table, but you should put an edge around it to stop the food from blowing off. Some people like to add a roof, but this is certainly not necessary. Position the table where you can see it from your window, but not right in the middle of the lawn: the birds like to stay fairly near the shelter of a hedge or bush. The table should be at least 1·5 metres high, so that cats cannot jump on to it. If you live in a town or city and have no suitable place to erect a standard bird table you might be able to fix a feeding tray to a wall or window sill.

Keep a record of all the birds that come to your table. Experiment with the food you provide and try to discover what sort of food each kind of bird prefers. A few birds, including the dunnock and the blackbird, prefer to take their food on the ground, so throw some of the food down for them.

Song Thrush

Dunnock

female
House Sparrow
Italian Sparrow (male) not found in Britain
male

Starling

female

Blackbird

Great Tit

male
Greenfinch

Robin

Blue Tit

House Martin

Magpie

summer
winter
Pied Wagtail

Swallow

City Birds

Blackbirds are especially fond of apples in the winter. Gradually cut down on feeding when the birds begin to nest in spring. There are plenty of natural foods around at this time and they are much better for the baby birds. Don't put out peanuts in the spring, but if you can get some mealworms from a pet shop your robin will be very grateful and may even take them from your hand.

Most birds like fruit, and you can encourage them into your garden by planting berry-bearing bushes such as cotoneasters and guelder roses. Honeysuckle also produces good fruits, and its flowers attract moths at night. Bushes also encourage birds to nest in your garden. Look at page 149 to discover how to make artificial homes for your garden birds as well.

City Birds

The birds that visit your garden can also be seen in town parks – which are really just big gardens. As long as there are some trees and bushes, you will find plenty of birds. But some birds manage to live right in the middle of our towns, where there is often no plant life of any kind. The best known of these city-dwellers is the town pigeon, shown on the page opposite. Watch how it struts along the pavements, pecking away at anything that looks as if it could be edible. This bird is not frightened of people and in some places, such as London's Trafalgar Square, you can see thousands of pigeons landing on tourists' hands and eagerly taking popcorn and any other food on offer.

Birds also gather around street markets, where lots of fruit and vegetable scraps fall to the ground. Railway stations and yards also provide plenty of food, accidentally dropped by passengers or spilt from grain wagons.

Town pigeons are descended from the wild rock dove that lives on rocky hillsides and sea cliffs. The rock dove has been domesticated

Below: A huge flock of starlings darkens the sky as it comes in to roost on a city's trees and buildings on a winter afternoon. If you live in the country watch out for small starling flocks linking up as they fly to the roost.

for centuries – for food, for racing or for show – and many birds inevitably escaped to take up residence in our towns. Millions now live in towns and cities nearly all over the world. Notice the great variation in colour, from the natural grey to black, brown and white: many are multicoloured. This variation is due to the many fancy varieties, bred by bird fanciers, that have escaped over the years to join the town flocks. Most birds still retain the natural pink patch on the neck and the white rump which you can see as they fly up. Listen to the call of the town pigeon: *oo-roo-cooooo*, with the last syllable loud and long. This is quite different from the *cu-coo-cu* of the collared dove (see page 124) which has a long middle syllable. The collared dove does not live in the middle of the town, but often mingles with the town pigeon in parks.

You won't have to search very hard to find the other major city bird, the house sparrow. This bird is essentially a seed-eater, but it thrives on all sorts of food that people may drop. The house sparrow is a little less common in city centres than it was in the days of horse-drawn transport, when the horses spilt grain all over the streets, but you can still see large numbers of these birds at railway yards and stations and around the docks. It makes its untidy nest in any convenient crevice. House sparrows are also abundant in parks and gardens. They are fond of company and usually move about in small flocks. The tree sparrow is similar to the house sparrow but the top of its head is brown. Look at the picture of the dunnock on page 125; can you see how this garden bird differs from the house sparrow? The large numbers of sparrows living in cities attract the kestrels. These speckled birds of prey sometimes nest on window sills and other high ledges in city centres.

On winter afternoons the city skyline may be darkened by huge flocks of starlings flying in to roost after a day spent feeding in gardens or open country. The flocks come from all directions and sleep together in their thousands. They use the same trees or buildings night after night and they are

The Aggressive Robin

Robins stake out their territories in the autumn and keep other robins out with their loud songs and aggressive behaviour. If you have a resident robin you can watch this behaviour by setting up a model robin. It need not be a very good model as long as it has a red breast. Your garden robin will attack it several times until it realizes that the model is harmless. Female robins move into the males' territories in the winter ready for nesting, but not without a few skirmishes.

The Town Pigeon

Town pigeons are quite happy to nest on buildings and even on statues, for these are not really very different from their original homes on the cliffs. Because their droppings disfigure buildings and monuments, their presence is not always welcome.

extremely noisy before they settle down. Their droppings also damage the trees and buildings. You won't see the flocks leave in the morning because the birds fly off singly or in small groups. It is thought that the extra warmth of the city attracts the starlings to these regular roosting places.

Garden Flowers

Garden Flowers

Have you ever wondered where our garden flowers and vegetables come from? You don't see them growing wild in the countryside. Many of them have been introduced from other countries: dahlias from Mexico, chrysanthemums from the Far East, and runner beans from South America. Many others are descended from native plants, but these may have changed so much that the original plants are no longer recognizable. Plant breeders used to take seeds from the biggest and brightest flowers each year, and gradually produced bigger and bigger flowers. They now pollinate the flowers of one variety with pollen from another to produce hybrids. These may look quite different from the original plants and it is difficult to say what their wild ancestors were. But you can see the resemblances in some cases: it is easy to see that the garden pansy has come from the little field pansy and the polyanthus still has many features in common with the wild primrose.

Garden Weeds

Weeds are simply plants growing where we don't want them. Some are foreign plants that have found their way over here and made a nuisance of themselves. Oxford ragwort, for example, is a native of Sicily and was taken to the Oxford Botanic Garden in the 18th century. Seeds soon escaped and the plant is now a common weed, especially in towns. It grows by the roadside as well as in gardens.

Most weeds, however, are native plants which prefer our well-dug and manured gardens to their natural homes on sand dunes, cliffs, and other steep rocks where fresh ground is always being exposed by land-slips. Many of the weeds are short-lived annuals which spring up from seed as soon as we dig our gardens. They scatter huge numbers of seeds and so there are always some ready to spring up. There are also some long-lived perennial weeds, such as the dock and the dandelion. The stinging nettle is another familiar perennial weed. Look at its stems and leaves under a hand lens to see the hairs that inject you with poison when you touch it.

Some common weeds are illustrated opposite. How many can you find in your garden? Explore your neighbourhood to see where they could have come from. If you live in a town, make a survey of a stretch of pavement or an old wall: look for weeds that have taken a foothold in cracks and crevices.

Plant Life on Walls

Explore old walls to find lichens – hardy little plants that often form circular patches on bricks and stones. Some are brightly coloured and people once collected them to make dyes for cloth. The lichens in the picture are map lichens, so called because their black-edged colonies often link up and then look like countries on a map. They occur in several different colours. Although lichens can grow in extremely cold and extremely hot and dry places, they cannot stand air pollution.

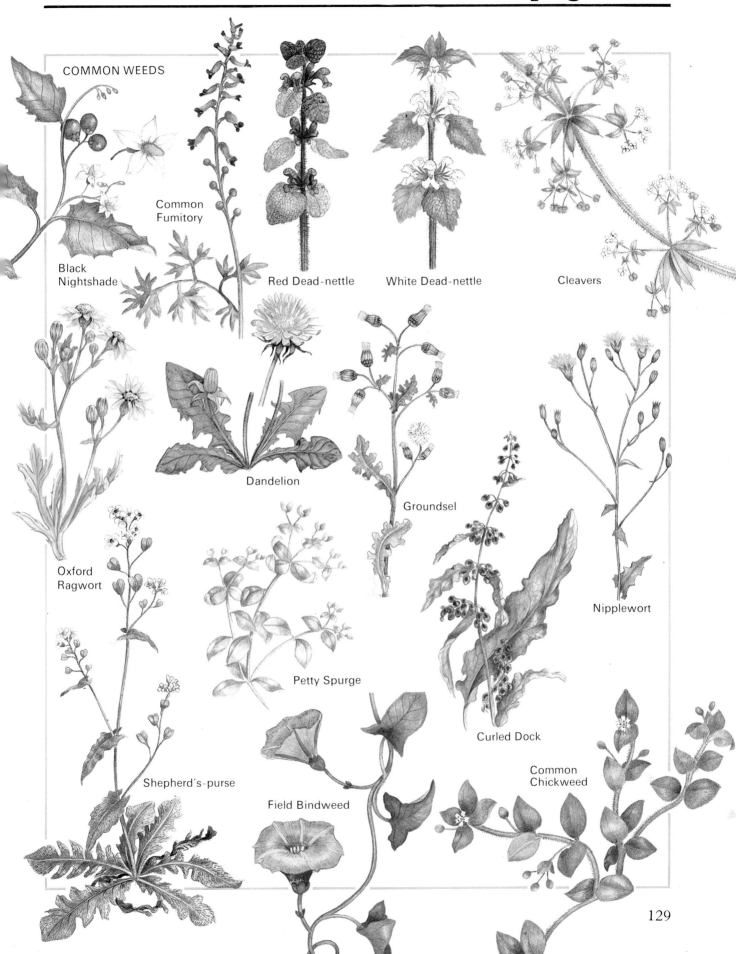

COMMON WEEDS

Black Nightshade

Common Fumitory

Red Dead-nettle

White Dead-nettle

Cleavers

Dandelion

Groundsel

Oxford Ragwort

Nipplewort

Petty Spurge

Curled Dock

Shepherd's-purse

Field Bindweed

Common Chickweed

Attracting Butterflies

A Butterfly Garden

No garden should be without the ice-plant, one of the best plants for attracting butterflies. Its domes of nectar-filled pink flowers open towards the end of summer and attract scores of butterflies, like the small tortoiseshells seen here with a red admiral. The small tortoiseshell sleeps through the winter and the ice-plant provides it with much of the food it needs to see it through this long sleep. A good butterfly garden will contain flowers from early spring until the last days of autumn, providing food for a wide range of butterflies.

Bring in the Butterflies

You can watch butterflies feeding at the flowers in the parks and gardens from early in the spring until well into the autumn. With the exception of the large and small whites, commonly known as cabbage whites, they are all welcome in the garden. As well as being beautiful to watch as they dance around the flowers, they help to pollinate the flowers, so that they produce seeds for the next year. Get as close as you can to some feeding butterflies and watch how they plunge their hair-like tongues into the flowers. The tongues are hollow and are used like drinking straws to suck up the sugary nectar. At the same time, pollen sticks on to the butterflies' legs and bodies and is carried from flower to flower. Watch how the butterfly coils its tongue up under its head when it has finished drinking.

A garden can be made especially attractive to butterflies by planting certain kinds of nectar-rich flowers. Aubretia is a good one for spring. Many people like to grow it on walls and in rock gardens. It is ideal for those butterflies that sleep through the winter and need food as soon as they wake up in the spring. Look out for small tortoiseshells, peacocks and brimstones on its flowers. Notice the very dark undersides of the tortoiseshells and peacocks. This helps to camouflage the insects during their winter sleep in hollow trees or in our sheds and attics. The brimstone prefers to sleep in a clump of ivy or a holly bush: see how its underside is green and leaf-like for good protection.

Good butterfly plants for later in the year include red valerian, lavender and the ice-plant pictured above. And don't forget the buddleia. This is often known as the butterfly bush, for its graceful purple flower spikes are thick with butterflies in the summer. Watch the butterflies closely to see what other kinds of flowers they like. They avoid the really big flowers because they can't reach the nectar. Notice how some species are happy to feed in large groups, while others prefer to be alone and tend to chase newcomers away.

You might like to try offering artificial foods to your garden butterflies. Put a solution of sugar and water in a bottle of the kind used for providing drinking water for pet mice (get this from your pet shop) and fix the bottle amongst the flowers. You may find butterflies feeding from it by day and moths by night.

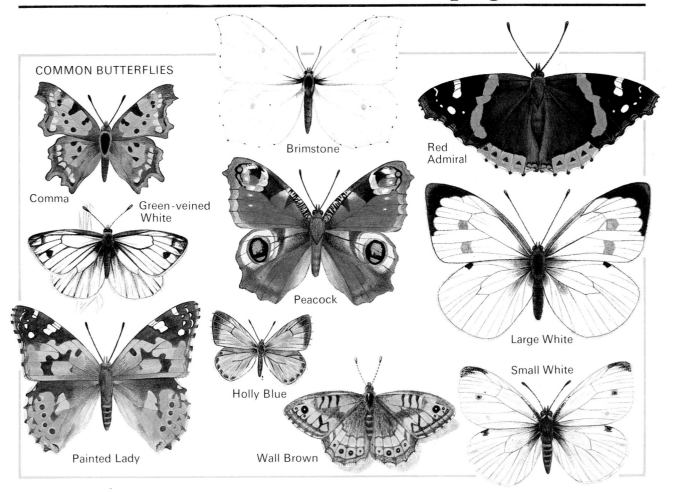

COMMON BUTTERFLIES

Comma

Brimstone

Red Admiral

Green-veined White

Peacock

Large White

Painted Lady

Holly Blue

Wall Brown

Small White

Some familiar garden butterflies are illustrated above. How many can you find in your garden or in your local park? Look at the comma's wings: they appear to have been torn, but the ragged appearance is quite natural. The underside is dark brown and the butterfly looks just like a dead leaf when it sleeps away the winter in the hedgerow. The green-veined white gets its name from the dark green lines on the underside. It is often blamed for destroying cabbages, but this is the work of its two cousins, the cabbage whites. The caterpillar of the green-veined white prefers to eat charlock, garlic mustard and other wild plants.

The Cabbage Whites
The large white butterfly looks very pretty as it sips nectar from the flowers, but its caterpillars destroy huge numbers of cabbages and related plants. Look for the clusters of yellow, skittle-shaped eggs under the leaves in August. The wise gardener will squash these eggs, but as a naturalist you might like to keep a batch to see what happens. The eggs hatch after a few days and the caterpillars start to feed. Give them fresh cabbage leaves every day and see how quickly they grow. Their strong smell and foul taste make them unacceptable to birds. After changing their skins several times they are ready to turn into pupae or chrysalises. They need upright surfaces for this and often choose fence posts or shed walls. Look for the speckled pupae in these places in the autumn. New butterflies emerge from them in the spring, but only a few ever get to this stage: most of the caterpillars are killed by parasitic insects which feed inside them. You will often find shrivelled caterpillars surrounded by the little yellow cocoons of these useful parasites.

The small white butterfly has a similar life history, but its caterpillars are green instead of black and yellow. They live singly while large white caterpillars spend their early life in dense colonies.

Bees and Wasps

The Buzzing of the Bees

As soon as the flowers open in spring they are visited by large furry bumble bees. These are queens that have just woken from their winter sleep. There are several different kinds: look for the different colour patterns. A few weeks later, when they have built up their strength on nectar, you will see them buzzing to and fro along the hedge bottoms in search of nesting sites on or under the ground. After a few weeks you will see some much smaller bees. These are the queens' first offspring, but they will not get any bigger. They are worker bees and they spend most of their time collecting pollen and nectar to feed bumble bee grubs back at the nest. Watch how they comb pollen from the body and pack it into the pollen baskets on the back legs: the baskets often bulge so much that the bees can hardly get airborne again. Don't be frightened to look closely: the bees won't hurt you.

The bumble bee is a social insect and several hundred adults may live in one nest.

Many other kinds of bees visit park and garden flowers and weeds, especially in spring. They are very important for pollinating the fruit trees. Most of them are solitary species, not living in large nests or colonies. Like the mason and digger wasps below, each female digs her own nest and provides food for her own young. There are no workers to look after the grubs as there are among the bumble bees and honey bees.

Watch the Wasps

Wasps also include both social and solitary species. The latter include many mason and digger wasps, but it is the social wasps that most of us notice in the garden, especially in late summer. Queen wasps appear a little later than bumble bee queens and they build their nests with paper which they make themselves

---

Bee and Wasp Nests

Mason Wasp    Digger Wasp

Small holes in brickwork are often the work of mason wasps, while digger wasps prefer to tunnel in the soil or in dead wood. The females of these insects work alone to dig out burrows for their young. Watch the entrance holes to see the insects bringing in small flies and other prey to stock their nests. Their grubs will eat this food later. Most of them take about a year to grow up and turn into new adults. The adults fly mainly in spring and summer.

Making a Bumble Bee Nest

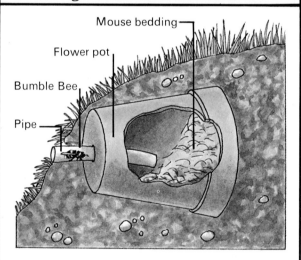

Mouse bedding
Flower pot
Bumble Bee
Pipe

Bumble bees often nest in old mouse holes. Encourage them to nest in your garden by providing an artificial home. All you need is a flower pot about 15 centimetres across, some old bedding from a pet mouse (or from a pet shop) and a piece of old pipe that fits the hole in the base of the pot. Bury the pot and bedding and poke through the pipe as shown above. With luck, a queen bee might find it a suitable place to build a nest.

by chewing wood into pulp. Their jaws scrape the wood from fence posts and many other objects, including dead hogweed stems, and it is quite a noisy business. You can hear it from several metres away on a still day.

The life history of the wasp colony is very much like that of the bumble bee colony, but the wasps feed their young on chewed-up insects instead of nectar and pollen. The wasps destroy lots of harmful insects during the summer, but they can become a nuisance themselves when their colonies break up in'

Above: Hover-flies are often mistaken for wasps because of their black and yellow coats. Even birds make this mistake and leave the hover-flies alone, although the flies are actually harmless. If you look closely you will see that the hover-fly has only two wings. Wasps have four.

Below: The Colorado beetle is a very serious pest of potato crops on the continent. It came originally from North America.

The Garden Greenfly

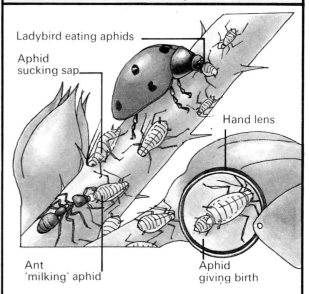

Ladybird eating aphids

Aphid sucking sap

Hand lens

Ant 'milking' aphid

Aphid giving birth

Examine the garden roses for greenfly in the spring. You are most likely to find these little insects, also known as aphids, clustering around the buds and young shoots. They dig their needle-like beaks into the plant and take out lots of sap for food. Most of the aphids are wingless in the spring, but you will find a few winged ones ready to fly to other plants. All are females at this time of the year and the adults can give birth to several babies every day. The young grow rapidly and soon have their own babies. In this way the aphid colony grows very quickly. Use your hand lens to look at the aphids and you might see one being born.

Several other insects live among the aphids. Ladybirds and their bluish grey grubs eat lots of them, but the aphids have their protectors as well. Look for ants roaming through the colony and stroking the aphids with their feelers. The ants are after honeydew, the sugary fluid which the aphids produce and which makes the plants sticky in the summer. The ants are so keen on the sweet honeydew that they guard the aphids and chase off intruders. Some ants even keep aphids like we keep cows. They take them into their nests and install them in special chambers with roots running through them. The aphids feed quite happily on the roots and when an ant wants a drink it merely goes up to an aphid and 'milks' it by stroking it gently.

Other Insects

the autumn. They spend their last few weeks feasting on ripe fruit and other sweet food. Notice how they fold their wings lengthwise, an easy way to distinguish the social wasps from the digger wasps. They may annoy you at the tea table, but they won't hurt you if you ignore them. Don't wave your arms around, for this will certainly make the wasps angry: and then they might sting. Like the queen bumble bee, the queen wasp sleeps through the winter and she wakes in the spring to form another colony.

Other Insects

Many people dislike earwigs, but these fierce-looking insects are quite harmless. They might nip with their pincers if you pick them up, but not hard enough to hurt you. They use the pincers to fight among themselves and also for defence against shrews and other animals that might try to eat them. The females have straighter and more slender pincers than the males. Earwigs are scavenging insects, eating almost anything when they come out at night. A good way to find them is to wrap an old cloth round the base of a tree trunk. The insects will congregate there and you can look at them in the morning.

Look out for the crane-flies or daddy-long-legs that are common in parks and gardens in late summer. They often buzz noisily around the house at night – try to catch one and examine it. Unlike most other insects, flies have only one pair of wings: the hind wings have been reduced to minute pin-like structures called balancers. They help the flies to fly straight. Notice that the male crane-fly has a swollen abdomen, while the female's is pointed at the tip. The females drive their abdomens into the ground to lay their eggs. Their grubs, known as leatherjackets, feed on the roots of grasses and other plants.

The Earthworm – a Valuable Friend

The famous naturalist Charles Darwin considered the earthworm to be one of the most important of all animals. It certainly plays a vital part in keeping the soil in good condition, and plants would not grow very well without it. There are thousands of worms in a hectare of soil, and they are especially common under grassland. Their tunnels help to drain the soil and provide air for plant roots. The animals also drag lots of dead leaves into the soil. Some of these are eaten but many are left to rot and enrich the

Life in a Forkful of Soil

Dig up a forkful of moist garden soil and examine it carefully on a board or a sheet of polythene. Some of the many kinds of animals that you might find in the soil are shown on the right. Wireworms are the grubs of slender beetles called click beetles. They eat plant roots and often tunnel into potatoes. Try spotting the difference between the carnivorous centipede and the vegetarian millipede by looking at the legs. Use a hand lens or magnifying glass to look for mites and other minute animals.

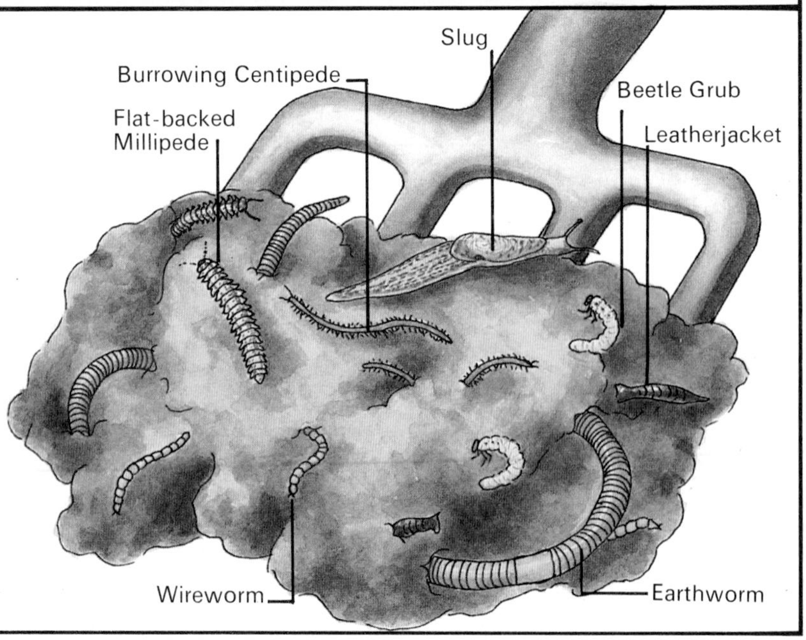

Slug
Burrowing Centipede
Beetle Grub
Flat-backed Millipede
Leatherjacket
Wireworm
Earthworm

soil. The worms also continuously mix the soil layers. They tunnel partly by swallowing the soil as they go and, after digesting any food material in it, they pass the soil out again as worm casts on or near the surface. In this way soil which has been swallowed in the deeper layers is regularly brought close to the surface. You can watch this ploughing action in a wormery like the one below. Only fine soil can be swallowed by the worms, and so in undisturbed places stones gradually sink as the worms take in soil from under them and deposit it on top.

Pick up a worm and try to work out which is its front end. Living in the soil, the animal has

Observing Snails

Trail can be made more visible by dusting with talcum powder

Snail rasping flesh from banana skin

Look for snails hiding in corners by day and mark their shells with blobs of paint. Search for them in the garden at night. How far have they travelled from home?

Making a Wormery

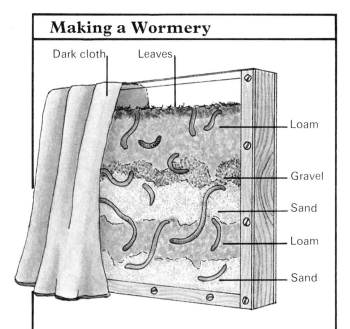

Dark cloth, Leaves, Loam, Gravel, Sand, Loam, Sand

This simple cage, consisting of two sheets of plastic about three centimetres apart in a wooden frame, will enable you to watch earthworms at work. Fill it with layers of different kinds of soil and add about six large worms. Drop some dead leaves or grass cuttings over the top as food for the worms and water well. Cover the wormery and examine it each day to see how the worms are getting on with their ploughing. Notice that the gravel layer gradually sinks as the worms remove the soil from beneath it. Look for worm casts on or near the surface of the soil.

no need of eyes. It doesn't even have a real head, but the front end is more pointed than the rear and the worm will usually try to move towards the front. Run your fingers along the underside of the worm – the paler surface – and feel the tiny bristles which give it a grip as it moves through its tunnels. The same bristles also anchor it firmly if you try to pull a worm from its tunnel. Put the worm on a piece of paper and you will hear the bristles scraping. Try putting it on a piece of glass. It won't be able to move because it cannot dig in its bristles.

Look for worms on the ground on humid nights in the summer. You might see them dragging leaves into their burrows. If you disturb them they will shoot rapidly backwards and disappear, for they always keep the rear end firmly anchored in the burrow.

Ants Everywhere

Most parks and gardens contain ants. You might see their nests when digging in the garden or moving stones, but these little insects are not usually very conspicuous. On one day of the year, however, the nests 'explode' as thousands of flying ants swarm out and take to the air. This is the ants' marriage flight and all the nests in a given area usually erupt at the same time. After mating, the males die. Most of the females also perish – many are eaten by birds and other predators – but some females survive and either go back

Ants and Spiders

Keeping Ants

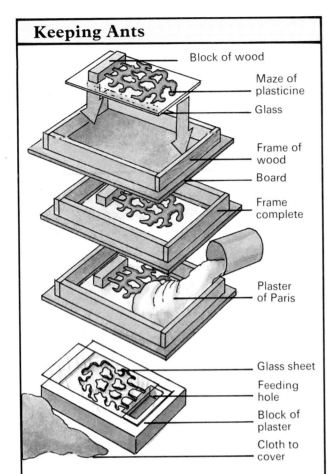

Block of wood

Maze of plasticine

Glass

Frame of wood

Board

Frame complete

Plaster of Paris

Glass sheet

Feeding hole

Block of plaster

Cloth to cover

Ants are easy to look after if you can make an escape-proof cage (formicarium) as shown above. Make sure the glass is about two centimetres smaller all round than the wooden frame: it should touch the frame only at the end opposite the wooden block. When the plaster has set, turn it upside-down and remove the wood and modelling wax. The plaster block now has a network of tunnels and a large hollow for a feeding area. Now go in search of ants. Wear gloves if you are after the red garden ants because these can sting. For a permanent colony you need the queen, who can be picked out by her much larger size. Put the ants in the formicarium and cover the tunnel area with a dark cloth. Slide the glass back a little to put fruit, honey and scraps of meat in the feeding area. Watch the ants come out to feed. Try giving them a stem thickly covered with aphids. Keep the tunnel area dark but examine it from time to time. Where does the queen take up residence to lay her eggs?

to their old nests to start laying eggs or they begin new colonies. Most of the ants in a colony are wingless workers. They are all daughters of the queen or queens and they do all the chores.

Our garden ants are omnivorous, eating lots of seeds and other plant matter as well as many other insects and other dead animals. But they are especially fond of sweet things and you will often see them collecting honeydew from aphids (see page 133). Put out some honey or a slice of orange in an area where you know there are ants. The workers will soon find it and you will see streams of them moving to and fro as they take the food back to the nest. Use a hand lens to watch the insects' jaws at work. There are two common garden species: the black ant, which even nests under town pavements, and the red ant. The black ant has no sting but the red ant, actually reddish-brown in colour, can give a painful sting.

Spiders in the Garden

Explore sunny flower beds and rockeries in spring and early summer and you may find small dark spiders sunbathing on the stones. These are wolf spiders. Instead of making webs, they chase after their insect prey. Try to catch one of the spiders in a glass tube. Look at it with your lens to see the large eyes – very necessary for a spider which relies on spotting prey from a distance and then running after it. You will sometimes see the females carrying their silken egg sacs at the rear end. When the eggs hatch the babies climb on to the mother's back and ride there for a few days, gradually falling off and becoming indepedent.

Many web-spinning spiders live in the garden. The garden spider, also known as the cross spider because of the markings on its back, is very common on bushes and fences. The webs that appear overnight on door and window frames usually belong to a greyish spider called *Zygiella x-notata*. Look closely at these webs and you will see that each has a triangular gap near the top. The spider hides in a nearby crevice and scampers down to the web when prey arrives. Try tickling the web with a piece of grass: you can sometimes fool the spider into thinking that its dinner has arrived – but not very often!

Life on a Wall

Brick and stone walls are readily colonized by animal life which takes to them just like natural rocks and cliffs. Old walls with soft and crumbling mortar are especially rich in wildlife because lots of plants can get a

Above: This Moorish gecko is a nocturnal lizard which hunts for insects on the walls in southern Europe. It often enters houses to hunt and can actually run across the ceiling. Notice its broad toes.

foothold here as well. Night is the best time for looking for animals on the wall, but keep your eyes open for the fascinating zebra spider in the sunshine. Its black and white pattern makes it hard to spot on lichen-covered walls. It is one of the jumping spiders, creeping slowly towards basking flies and then leaping on to them like a cat. Enormous eyes help it to judge distance very accurately. Search for the web of the spider *Segestria senoculata*: look carefully, for there is not much to see. The spider hides in a crevice and surrounds its lair with a number of trip-threads spreading out like the spokes of a wheel. When an insect stumbles over one of the threads the spider rushes out to catch it.

For night observations equip yourself with a strong torch. Woodlice are often very common on walls at night. Their skins are not waterproof and, like many other small animals, they come out at night because the air is moister then and there is less risk of drying up. In dry weather they keep nearer to the ground. Try to discover whether moonlight has any effect on them: do they stay lower down on moonlit nights? The woodlice feed on algae, pollen grains and other vegetable debris.

Life on a Wall

Old walls are very good places for finding small animals, especially if you look for them with a torch at night. Snails and woodlice browse on the algae and mosses, together with a host of very tiny insects. Numerous spiders make their homes in the crevices and either snare insects with webs or rush out to grab them. The long-legged house centipede also feeds on small insects. It lives mainly in the warmer parts of Europe but sometimes occurs in houses further north.

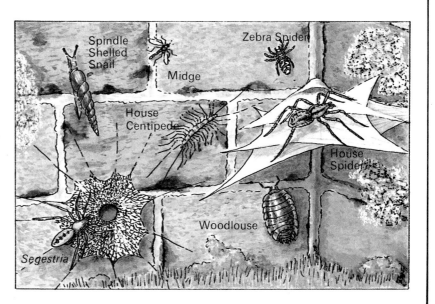

The Garden at Night

Centipedes hunt on the walls at night, catching flies and other insects that take a rest there. In southern Europe keep an eye open for the long-legged, speedy house centipede. It often comes indoors. You might even find scorpions hiding in crevices with their claws poking out to sieze passing prey.

Harvestmen are very common in the autumn, striding over the walls on their long legs and pouncing on a variety of small animals. They look rather like spiders, but if you study them carefully you will see that their bodies are not divided into two sections like the spiders. Harvestmen make no webs and have no poisonous fangs.

Observing at Night

As the sun sets in the evening, the butterflies seek shelter and the moths start to wake up. By dusk in the summer there are hundreds of moths floating and skimming through the garden. Take a torch and watch them feeding at the flowers. Some settle to take the nectar, while others may hover and feed with the aid of very long tongues. Some moths do not feed at all as adults, putting all their efforts into finding mates. Some familiar moths of parks and gardens are pictured below. The silver-Y flies in the daytime as well as by night. The eyed hawkmoth is well camouflaged when at rest on tree trunks by day, but if you disturb it it flashes the eye-like patterns on its hind wings. This frightens small birds, which think that the 'eyes' belong to a cat or an owl. You can find moths at all times of the year, but only a few are about in the winter.

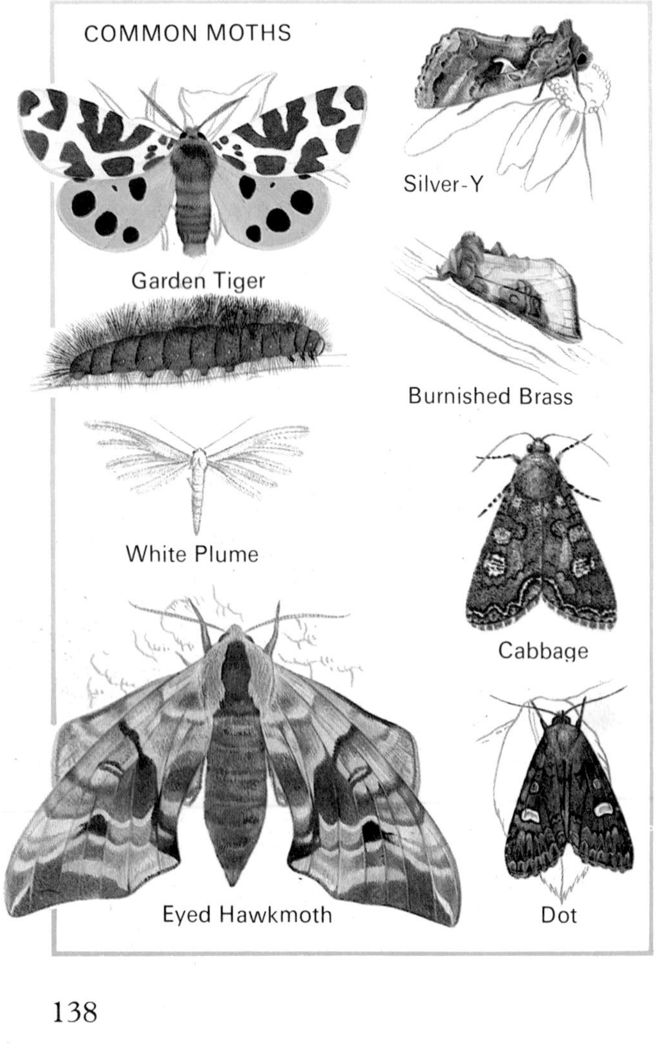

Most moths are attracted to bright lights such as street lamps. Look at the lamps in your street on summer and autumn evenings and watch the moths crash to the ground or settle on nearby walls. Quite a number will come to your window if you leave the light on and the curtains undrawn. People who study moths make use of this attraction by putting out light-traps. These usually contain mercury-vapour lamps which give out lots of ultra-violet light. We can't see the ultra-violet, but moths certainly can. They spiral in to the lamp and fall through a funnel into the trap below. They can't escape and the entomologist – insect expert – can examine them and release them in the morning. You can buy a trap like this or make one: fix a strong light to a thin piece of wood and place this across a funnel poked into a cardboard box. If you can't make or buy a trap, try hanging a bright lamp over a white sheet. A camping light is ideal for this, but the beauty of a trap is that you can find out what moths visit your garden without staying up all night.

COMMON MOTHS

Garden Tiger

Silver-Y

White Plume

Burnished Brass

Cabbage

Eyed Hawkmoth

Dot

Acrobatic Bats

Bats start to fly at sunset and they catch huge numbers of moths and beetles during the night. Watch their amazingly agile flight as they twist and turn after insects against the darkening sky. They are the only mammals that can really fly. Their wings consist of flaps of skin running along the sides of the body and stretched across the incredibly long fingers. The bats are not blind, but their eyesight is poor and they rely on their powerful hearing to find their way and to catch food. As they plunge through the air they send out high-pitched sounds and listen for the echoes bouncing back from nearby objects. They know when the echoes are coming back from an insect and they change course to catch it. The insect is sometimes caught in the bat's mouth, but moths are more often scooped up in the wings.

Bats spend the daytime asleep, hanging upside-down in hollow trees, old buildings, roof spaces and similar places. Some even sleep amongst thick ivy. Our European bats, of which there are about 30 species, all go into hibernation through the winter months when there are simply not enough moths and other insects on the wing for them to eat.

The Hedgehog

The hedgehog is essentially a mammal of the hedgerow and the woodland edge but it finds our parks and gardens very much to its liking. It is a very common animal in many suburban areas. It spends the daytime asleep in rubbish heaps or in a leafy bed at the bottom of a hedge and comes out to feed at night. Together with the mole and the shrew, it belongs to a group known as the insectivores or insect-eaters, but it actually eats almost anything. It is very fond of earthworms and of the slugs and beetles that roam our gardens at night. Hedgehog droppings – often the first clue to the animals presence – are long and black and often full of beetle legs and wing-cases. There may also be pieces of centipede and earwig skeletons. Fruit is another important part of the hedgehog's diet, especially in the autumn when ripe fruit falls to the ground.

Above: A bat in flight. Notice the very long fingers supporting the wings. Notice also the large ears used for picking up the echoes, and the sharp insect-crushing teeth.

Right: Hedgehogs are good climbers. This one, showing its remarkably pig-like snout, has climbed a garden wall. To come down again it will just roll into a ball and drop to the ground. Notice there are no prickles underneath.

Garden Animals

Our lawns make fine courting grounds for the hedgehog. You might well have been woken up by the noisy performance in spring and summer as the male stomps round and round the female with much loud snorting and squealing. If you suspect that you have hedgehogs in or around your garden, try putting out some food for them. A bowl of cereal with some milk and dried fruit is ideal. The animals also like cat food. They are easy to watch and will come back night after night for food. Don't be tempted to take them indoors because they are loaded with fleas: the spines prevent them from grooming themselves like other animals.

Rats and Mice

The rats and mice belong to the large group of animals called rodents. They have chisel-like front teeth with which they can gnaw through all sorts of materials. The common or brown rat and the house mouse both came from Asia originally but are now found nearly all over the world. Both are very common in urban areas, indoors as well as out, and they do a lot of damage to food and other stores. In country areas these pests are found mainly around farms and rubbish dumps, although

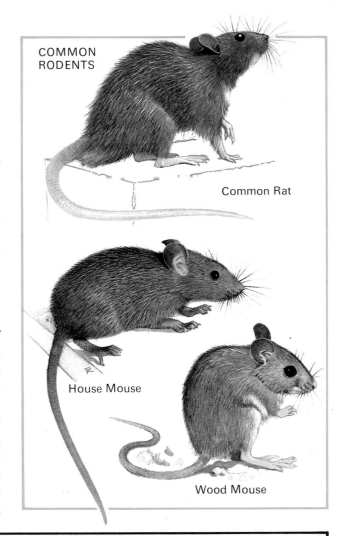

COMMON RODENTS

Common Rat

House Mouse

Wood Mouse

The Longworth Trap

The Longworth trap catches small mammals without hurting them. When the animals step on the trip-wire, the door drops down and imprisons them. Put some newspaper or other bedding in the trap to keep the animals warm at night. Bait is not necessary, but you can add some bread or grain and shrews will appreciate a lump of meaty cat food. Remember to check the trap regularly so that the animals do not go hungry. Release them after examination if you have nowhere to keep or feed them (see page 30).

Entrance tunnel

Nesting chamber

Tripwire holding up door

Above: Foxes commonly come into gardens to look for food, even in the middle of towns. They often raid dustbins and this one has leapt on to a bird table in search of its supper.

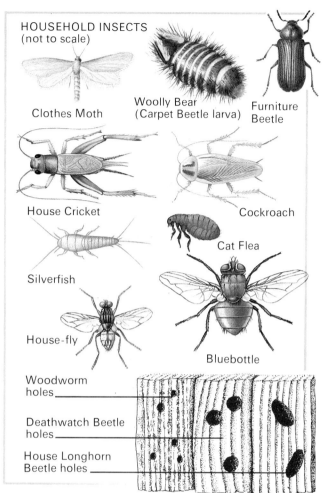

HOUSEHOLD INSECTS
(not to scale)

Clothes Moth

Woolly Bear
(Carpet Beetle larva)

Furniture
Beetle

House Cricket

Cockroach

Silverfish

Cat Flea

House-fly

Bluebottle

Woodworm
holes

Deathwatch Beetle
holes

House Longhorn
Beetle holes

the rat can travel many miles through open country, especially along river banks.

The wood mouse often lives in gardens, in towns as well as in country areas, and often comes into houses where there are no house mice to compete with it. It has larger eyes and ears and much larger feet than the house mouse. Woodmice generally nest just under the ground and make runways all over their territories. Look for their food stores in and under sheds and in log piles. The stores contain various nuts, cherry pips, dried hawthorn fruits and assorted seeds. By the end of winter most of these stores have been used up and only empty shells remain.

Insects in the House

The illustrations above right show a few of the many insects that can be found in houses and other buildings. You will find many more if you search cupboards and neglected corners. Some, like the small flies that swarm over the window panes, are accidental prisoners, but many others take up permanent residence in our buildings and do a great deal of harm. The grubs of clothes moths and carpet beetles chew through woollen clothes and carpets. Cockroaches and crickets eat all kinds of foods. The cat flea sucks blood from our household pets and often has a go at us as well. Bluebottles and houseflies both carry disease germs to food. Bluebottles also lay their eggs on meat and fish and their grubs quickly eat through the food. Silverfish are primitive wingless insects covered with minute silvery scales. Try picking one up – if you can catch it – and you will find the scales all over your fingers. These insects feed on spilt flour and other scraps and don't do much harm, although they sometimes damage books and wallpaper.

Even rafters, floor boards and wooden furniture are not safe from insect attack. The grubs of the furniture beetle or woodworm chew through all kinds of wood and the adult beetles leave the familiar tell-tale holes as they leave. By then the damage has been done.

Garden Ponds

Making a Garden Pond

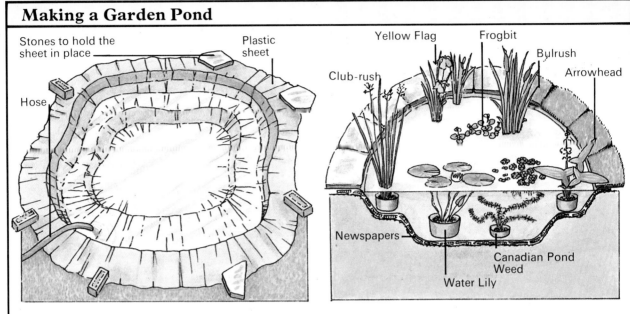

Use black polythene or a special pond liner to make a pond of any shape you like. Dig the hole to a depth of at least 75 centimetres in the centre and leave a shallow ledge around the edge. Put a layer of newspaper or soft sand in the bottom to protect the liner from any sharp stones and then stretch the liner across the hole. Hold the edges down with a few large stones and then start to fill your pond. Watch the liner gradually stretch and mould itself to the shape of the hole. The plants are best kept in pots. Put the ones that like shallow water on the ledges. Finish off the edge with stone or turf, making sure that you have an area of sloping bank where newts and other creatures can crawl out.

Deathwatch beetles don't normally invade ordinary houses. They like very old oak and are most often found in churches. In the wild these beetles all play a useful role in getting rid of dead trees

A Garden Pond

Garden ponds can be a lot of fun for the naturalist, and are very important for wildlife. As streams become polluted and many old farm and village ponds are filled in, garden ponds are taking over as major homes for frogs and toads and many other water-loving animals. Try to get a pond installed in your garden. It is not a difficult job. You can buy ready-shaped glass fibre ponds which are merely dropped into holes dug to the same shape. Alternatively, you can use a flexible liner as shown above. The pond need not be very large, but try to make it at least a metre across. Planted with a variety of native water plants, it will soon look quite natural. Buy your plants from a garden centre or get them from pond-owning friends: never dig them up from the wild.

Frogs, toads and newts will all find your pond and may well breed there. Many water-loving insects will also set up home in the pond. Look for water beetles scurrying amongst the submerged plants and coming up for air every now and then. Pond skaters may skim about on the surface, darting about after small flies that fall into the water. Watch the water snails gliding over the plants. They help to keep down the fluffy green algae that build up around the sides of the pond, but too many snails will destroy the pond plants. Dragonflies may swoop to and fro over a fairly large pond, streaking after the small midges that congregate there. Swallows and martins may even come to gather mud for nest-building. You can add goldfish if you like, but they will eat many of the other animals. They may themselves be eaten by a visiting heron.

The Naturalist at Work

As soon as you start to explore the world outside you will meet hundreds of different kinds of plants and animals and you will want to know the names of some of them. The larger and more colourful things, including trees, mammals and birds, and most flowers and butterflies, can be identified quite easily with the help of good guide books.

But guide books can't tell you everything and the best way to get to know your local countryside and its wildlife is to join your local natural history society or naturalists' trust. These groups normally organize excursions, during which you can explore under the guidance of expert naturalists. You will be able to learn the names of the plants and animals around you, and also pick up lots of tips on how to identify things from brief glimpses or even just snatches of songs.

A Better View

You don't need a lot of equipment for exploring the countryside, but most naturalists find that they need binoculars sooner or later, especially if they are studying birds or mammals. There are many models on the market and it is important to choose a pair that suits your particular purpose. If you look at a pair of binoculars you will see two numbers marked on them: 8 x 30 is a typical example, indicating that the binoculars magnify things eight times and that the objective lenses – those furthest from your eyes – are 30 millimetres in diameter. The size of the objective lenses has nothing to do with the magnification of the binoculars, but it does control the amount of light passing through them. Small objectives allow less light through than large ones and binoculars of this type are therefore not very good in dim light. If you want to watch birds or mammals at dusk or at night you should choose a pair with large objectives.

Binocular magnifications generally range from about x 6 – the smallest to be of any real use – to about x 12. You might be tempted to go for the highest magnification, but this is a mistake unless you are interested only in seabirds or mountain animals, which are usually a long way away. Powerful binoculars cannot be focused on objects less than about

The Home Laboratory

You will undoubtedly collect all kinds of specimens while exploring the countryside – pressed flowers, bark rubbings, sea shells and many other oddments. You will also have various pieces of equipment, including your binoculars. It is a good idea to keep all these things together. Try to get a table or desk specially for this purpose – a sort of home laboratory where you can study your collections. A good light is necessary, especially if you are using a microscope. The same light can be used for warming a vivarium if you have one.

Binoculars and Microscopes

eight metres away, and so you might not be able to study the birds on your bird table. Until recently, powerful binoculars were also large and heavy and very tiring to carry around all day. Improvements in design have overcome this problem, but powerful light-weight binoculars are still rather expensive. The ordinary naturalist can manage perfectly well with less powerful equipment. Always choose the best you can afford within the size and magnification range that you need (see above), and make sure that you try the binoculars before buying them. Do they feel comfortable at your eyes? Are they too heavy to carry for long periods? Do they focus smoothly? Take them outside the shop and focus on buildings at different distances. Is everything sharp and clear?

A Closer Look

If you want to study the smaller plants and animals, or to make a detailed examination of flowers, you will certainly need some kind of magnifying glass. The most convenient kind for use in the countryside is a hand lens. You can buy these pocket lenses quite cheaply, with a choice of magnifications. For general use a x10 lens is the most suitable. Use it together with good guide books and it will help you to identify numerous insects, spiders, mosses and other small organisms. Tie your lens to a piece of string and keep it round your neck while you are out: it will be easy to get at and you won't leave it behind.

Below: Using a simple hand lens to study the structure of a clover flower-head. You will be surprised how much detail it reveals.

Choosing a Microscope

A microscope is not essential for the amateur naturalist, but it will enable you to identify many small creatures, especially those living in soil and leaf litter. Like the hand lens, it also opens up a world of beautiful and complex patterns and amazing detail. If you are lucky enough to have a microscope you will undoubtedly spend many hours gathering and gazing at insects and other small animals, shells, leaves and an assortment of sand grains and other materials.

Microscopes are of two main kinds: monocular microscopes, with a single eye-piece, and binocular microscopes with two eye-pieces. Monocular microscopes generally magnify things 100 times or more and are used mainly for examining minute pieces of animals or plants. A simple microscope of this kind costs only a few pounds and would make a nice birthday present. Binocular microscopes are more expensive but you can sometimes find second-hand ones. Low-power binocular microscopes, magnifying about 30 times, have the advantage of space between the body of the microscope and the object you are looking at. You can even examine live insects under it – something that you can't do with a monocular model unless the animals are extremely small.

Photographing Nature

Most naturalists like to take photographs of the various sorts of countryside and of the plants and animals that live there. It is the ideal way to build up a record of the changes occurring in a particular place from season to season and, if done carefully, it causes no

The Binocular Microscope

Binocular microscopes with a magnification of between 30 and 50 times are ideal for looking at and identifying small insects. The distance between the microscope and the object means you can use tweezers or a needle to move legs and wings or to turn the whole animal over. Always work in a good light when using a microscope.

harm to the plants and animals. The wildlife photographer normally chooses a single-lens reflex camera with a detachable lens. The reflex arrangement, consisting of a mirror and various prisms, allows you to see *exactly* what the camera lens is seeing, so that you can compose your picture properly without chopping off the top of a flower or the head of an animal. The detachable lens allows you to put extension tubes between it and the camera body for close-up pictures, and also allows you to use different lenses for different effects. A telephoto lens, for example, works like a telescope, enlarging part of the view so that objects come out larger in the final picture. A wide-angle lens works the other way: each object appears smaller in the final picture but, because the lens covers a wider field, you get much more of the landscape in your picture.

A complete outfit for wildlife photography is very expensive, but you don't have to buy everything at once. Decide on one of the well-known makes of 35 mm SLR cameras and then you can build up your outfit gradually, getting thoroughly familiar with each piece of equipment as you get it. If possible, choose a camera with a built-in exposure meter which

Below: Binoculars are not just for looking at distant objects. Here they are being used to watch large spiders on the far side of a ditch.

measures the amount of light actually coming through the lens. The camera will then indicate the right exposure no matter what lens or other attachment you are using, but there is one important thing to remember if you are photographing scenes with lots of sky or snow in them. The exposure meter will be unduly affected by the bright areas and the landscape will come out too dark unless you adjust the camera setting.

To start with, all you need is the camera body equipped with a standard lens and a skylight filter. The filter is especially important in the mountains or by the sea, where there is lots of ultra-violet light. Without it, the ultra-violet gets through to the film and makes the pictures too blue. A standard lens is fine for general landscapes, trees, groups of flowers and large animals. A sturdy tripod

should be high on your list. It holds the camera steady and allows you to make long exposures without risk of camera-shake. This is especially useful in landscape photography, where the long exposure and small aperture give you sharpness throughout the picture.

The next most useful piece of equipment is a telephoto lens. Using the standard lens, a sparrow photographed from only three metres away would still fill only a very small part of your picture. A 200 mm telephoto lens is useful for photographing birds on a bird-table, but for birds in the wild you really need a lens of at least 400 mm focal length.

Taking Close-ups

If you want to photograph insects or take close-ups of flowers you will need some close-up accessories. Extension tubes, which fit between the lens and the camera body, are the most convenient. You will usually find that you need extra light for close-up photography, and this means attaching a small electronic flash. Many photographers prefer two flashes linked together so that they fire

Above left: Flowers, photographed with a large aperture to throw the surroundings out of focus.

Left: Wide-angle lenses are good for scenery as they take in a large area. The photograph, left, was taken with a 35 mm lens and includes the stream as well as the mountain. The picture above was taken from exactly the same spot, but with a 200 mm telephoto lens. This acts like a telescope, magnifying just a small part of the scene – in this case the heather in the centre.

Wildlife Photography

Right: The author at work on a close-up photograph of a flower using a simple flash-gun to provide extra light. Two or even three flash-guns are sometimes required for certain pictures. You might have to get into very awkward positions to take close-up pictures, but always take care not to damage surrounding vegetation.

Speeds and Stop Numbers

Cameras normally have two movable rings engraved with numbers. Together, they control the amount of light entering the camera. Too little or too much light falling on the film will spoil the picture. One ring controls the speed at which the shutter opens and closes, and in a typical camera it may range from half a second to 1/500th second. Don't use speeds slower (longer) than 1/60th second without a tripod or you may get blurred pictures through camera shake. The second ring controls the size of the aperture through which light gets into the camera. It is generally marked from about 2·8 to 16 or 22. The larger the number, the smaller the aperture. A small aperture gives a good depth of field, with everything nice and sharp from the foreground into the far distance. To make up for the small aperture, however, you must give a longer exposure so that the right amount of light reaches the film. A large aperture gives only a shallow depth of field: if the foreground is in focus the background will be blurred, and vice-versa. This is often useful if you want to make a bird or a flower stand out from the background. Large apertures go with short exposures, and the latter are also needed to 'freeze' moving subjects.

simultaneously. This reduces the shadows caused by a single flash. You can achieve a similar result with a sheet of white paper on one side to reflect the light into the shadow areas. Unless you have the very latest automatic equipment, you must experiment at first to find out just how far away the flash must be for the correct exposure. In all close-up photography you must work with small apertures to get enough depth of field.

Remember the Rules

Naturalists and photographers have devised a set of rules for wildlife photography. Designed to protect our wildlife, these rules can be summed up by stating that the welfare of the subject is more important than the photograph. Remember this when you are photographing plants and animals. Don't trample on other flowers to get a good picture of one specimen, and don't pull up plants that might be in your way – although you can certainly bend the stalks gently out of the way while taking your pictures: tent pegs are useful for holding grasses back in this way. Leave the place as you found it, and always ask permission if you want to photograph something on private land. Remember that it is against the law to disturb nesting birds.

147

Watching Birds and Mammals

A Hide for Watching Birds

Most wild birds are shy and timid and it is difficult to watch them properly without some kind of camouflage. If they can't see you they will act normally and may come quite close. It is sometimes sufficient to hide behind trees and bushes, but these are not always available. Bird photographers, who often have to sit for hours or even days to get their pictures, make artificial hides – sometimes very elaborate ones high in the trees.

Making a Hide

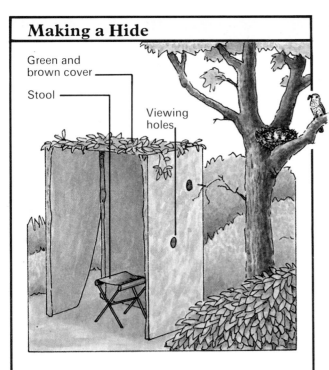

Green and brown cover

Stool

Viewing holes

Make a frame from eight strong canes or straight branches lashed together with string at the top. Cut an old sheet painted green and brown into two rectangles and sew them together into a large bag to fit neatly over the top and sides. Sew in a piece of plastic under the top to make it waterproof and make a flap in one side for an entrance. Cover the hide with a few leafy branches for extra camouflage and make peepholes in one side at the right height for comfortable viewing. Make one for your camera if you want to take photographs. The hide shown here is cut away to show the interior with its folding stool. If watching a nest, make sure that you don't disturb the birds while setting up your hide.

For everyday bird-watching, you can make a simple hide with a couple of stout canes and an old sheet dyed or painted brown and green to match the surroundings. Fix the sheet to the canes and sit or stand behind it. This is a very practical hide if you want to watch birds in a particular spot – birds coming to and from a nest box, for example.

But if you want to watch birds all around you, a hide like the one on the left is necessary. Such a hide is ideal for regular bird-watching in a large garden or on other private land where it can be left in position so that the birds get used to it. Farmers and other land owners are usually quite happy for you to set up a hide on their land, but remember to ask their permission first. Unfortunately, you can't leave a hide safely in parks or on commons and other public spaces, and you can't rebuild it every time you want to use it because this would frighten the birds away. The answer here is to use a mobile hide, carried in front of you like a shield. A folding clothes airer with a camouflaged sheet draped over it works quite well, but you can make a lighter frame with a few strips of wood. The hide can be erected in an instant with no disturbance to the surroundings, and you can also creep forward with it.

Hides and Mammals

You can also use your hide to observe mammals, such as deer, although hides are not really necessary for mammal-watching. Mammals generally have poorer eyesight than birds and, as long as you keep still, they probably won't notice you. The advantage of a hide is that you can shuffle about behind it without disturbing the animals. The really important thing is to be downwind of the animals, so that the wind does not carry your scent or your sounds to them: most mammals rely on scents and sounds to warn them of danger. The mobile hide is obviously the one to use, because you can then adjust your position according to the wind direction. Get to know the habits of your local deer: they usually follow definite routes each day and have favourite resting places, and when you have discovered these you will be able to watch them much more easily. Look for their characteristic footprints, known as slots, to show you where the deer gather.

A Nest Box for your Garden

If you have enjoyed feeding the birds in your garden in the winter, encourage some of them to stay around for the spring and summer by putting up a few nest boxes. You can buy ready-made boxes from pet shops and garden centres, or you can make them yourself. Don't worry about a few gaps or rough edges. The gaps will actually aid ventilation.

The tit-box, with a small hole in the side or front, is the most popular kind of nest box. You can make one from a log or from a single plank of wood (see right). Such a box will attract blue tits, coal tits and great tits. Tree sparrows, nuthatches and tree creepers will also move into nest boxes of this kind, and if you make sure that the entrance hole is no more than 29 millimetres across you will keep out the house sparrow. The birds that use these boxes normally nest in holes in the tree trunks, and so you need not hide the nest box away in the branches. You can fix it to a tree trunk or a fence or a wall so that you can get a good view of the birds, but it must be out of the reach of cats and not in the full sun. The box need not be on a vertical surface, but if it does slope make sure that the entrance faces downwards so that the rain does not get in. Robins, spotted flycatchers and many other small birds prefer open-fronted boxes, sited in more protected places, such as walls or tree trunks covered with climbing plants.

If you have a suitable shed or fence you might be able to set up an observation nest box. This is made from a plank in the normal way, but the back is made from a sheet of clear glass or plastic and the box is then fitted against a hole in the shed or fence so that you can look through the back.

All nest boxes should be in position well before the nesting season so that the birds can explore them thoroughly and get used to them. Watch the birds choosing their homes and gathering nesting material for them.

Making a Nest Box

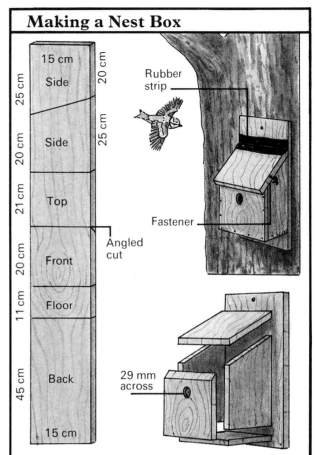

To make a tit-box, you will need a plank of wood, a strip of rubber inner tube, some nails or screws and a fastener. Cut the plank into two sections as shown in the diagram. Drill an entrance hole (29 mm in diameter) in the front section and a few small drainage holes in the floor section. Nail the strip of rubber to the lid and back to form the hinge and then nail or screw the sections together. Fit the catch to the side. An open-fronted nest box can be made in the same way but it needs only half of the front section and no hinged lid.

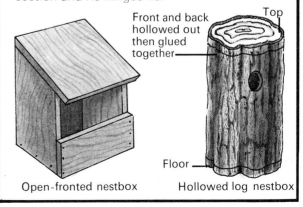

Open-fronted nestbox   Hollowed log nestbox

A simple Vivarium

Don't be tempted to open the boxes to see how the birds are getting on: the hinged lids are for cleaning out the boxes in the autumn.

Remember that most birds are strongly territorial in the breeding season, with each pair defending a particular area. A small garden is not likely to support more than one pair of each kind, so don't waste your money on lots of boxes: two tit-boxes and two open-fronted kinds are plenty for a small garden.

A Simple Vivarium

A vivarium is merely an artificial home for land animals, just as an aquarium is a home for water-living creatures. You can use it as a temporary home for many of the animals that you find in the countryside, and you can have a lot of fun watching them before setting them free again. Mice, voles, frogs and toads will all be happy in your vivarium for a few days, and so will lizards – if you can catch them. Crickets and grasshoppers will also entertain you with their chirping.

You must be sure that you can provide the right kind of food for your 'pets' before you go to the trouble of setting up your vivarium. Grasshoppers are easy to feed; they need only a bunch of fresh grass each day. Voles will also eat grass, and mice will eat bread and biscuits and scraps from the table. Frogs and toads are

A Temporary Home for Watching Animals

Vivaria are often sold in pet shops, but these tend to be made of metal and they are not really suitable because it is not easy to see what is happening inside. An old fish tank makes a very good vivarium, and it doesn't matter if it leaks. Fit a cover of perforated zinc or fine wire mesh. Strong wooden boxes can be used if you turn them on their sides and put a glass or plastic window across the front. They also need ventilation panels made of perforated zinc. You can often find old cupboards in junk shops which may be right for conversion to vivaria. The best size is about 50 centimetres long, 30 centimetres wide and 50 centimetres high. This vivarium houses frogs and toads.

more difficult to feed. You will need lots of insects and slugs to keep them happy, although you might be able to tempt them with small pieces of fresh meat dangled on pieces of thread. The maggots sold for fishing bait are a good form of insect food.

How you furnish your vivarium depends very much on what animals you are going to keep. Lizards need a layer of gravel on the bottom and a few logs or rocks on which to bask. A small dead branch will give them something else to scamper over, and the animals might like a small piece of turf to explore. You can put a fresh piece of turf in every week or two. Drinking water is important and can be provided in a small pond made from a shallow pie dish. A similar set-up will satisfy mice and voles, but arrange the rocks or logs to form a sleeping chamber. Give voles lots of turf to nibble and tunnel in.

Frogs and toads require moister conditions and you should cover the gravel with a layer of damp peat or moss. Give them a fair-sized pool to bathe in. If your vivarium is made from a fish tank and still holds water, you can put an inch or two in the bottom and then build up the rocks and branches, but this arrangement is less easy to clean out than one in which the 'pond' is in a separate dish. It is very important to keep the vivarium clean.

Frogs, toads and lizards will appreciate some extra warmth, which you can provide by shining a reading lamp into the vivarium for a few hours each day. A 40-watt lamp is sufficient for the animals to 'sunbathe'. Grasshoppers will sing more when it is warm.

Simple Sound Recording

If you have a small cassette tape recorder you can try making recordings of birds and other animals, including grasshoppers and crickets. A tape recorder with a manual recording level control will produce better results than one with an automatic control. The slender stick microphones that come with most cassette recorders are quite good, but you will get better results with a slightly more expensive microphone. Be sure to get a low impedance microphone, which will allow you to use a

Sound Recording

Before making a sound recording, identify the animal you are recording and look for the best possible position to record it from without disturbing it. Here a cricket in a tree is being recorded with a simple microphone tied to a stick. The microphone is shielded from wind noise by gauze wrapped around a wire frame. This creates a zone of still air around the microphone. Hides are useful for recording birds and other animals.

long lead and get the recorder well away from the microphone. Then you won't hear the hum of the motor. Try not to hold the microphone in your hand, for it will pick up the slightest movement of your fingers: it is a good idea to bind or clip the microphone to a long stick. Always use headphones to hear exactly what you are picking up.

When using a stick microphone you usually have to put it very close to the sound you are recording. Try attaching it to a bird table in the garden: with a long lead you can hide indoors and listen to what is happening. Or put your microphone in a flower bed to pick up the sounds of the visiting bees. Add a brief commentary after each item so that you will not forget what each recording is.

Bats and Moths

Make a Bat-box

You've probably seen bats flitting rapidly through the air at dusk, but few people ever get close enough to see what the animals really look like. If you put up a bat-box you may be lucky enough to be able to watch these fascinating creatures at close quarters.

The bat-box looks rather like the tit-box on page 149, but the entrance is a slit in the floor. If you leave a gap about 15 mm wide between the back and the floor most kinds of bat will be able to get in. Use rough timber and make the box about 10 cm square and 20 cm high. Leave a good 15 cm of the back projecting below the floor so that the bats have plenty of room when they land at the front door. Don't use preservatives on the wood. Bats don't like the smell and the preservatives could even kill them. Fix the box on a tree or a wall at least 2 m above the ground and preferably as high as 5 m.

Many bats are becoming rare and boxes like this can help them to become common again, but you must never disturb the animals. Use binoculars to watch them stretching their wings and flying out in the evening. If you get up early, you can also watch them returning at dawn. It's a good idea to put the box where you can see it from your bedroom window. A south-facing box is most likely to be used for summer roosting, while one on a north-facing tree or wall is preferred for the long winter sleep.

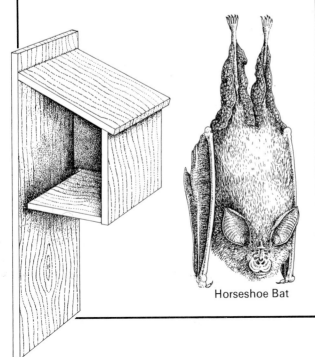

Horseshoe Bat

Make a Simple Moth Trap

A sturdy cardboard box can be used to make a perfectly good moth trap for your garden. You will also need a plastic funnel about 25 cm wide across the top. Cut the lower part of the funnel away so that the opening is about 6 cm across and then cut a circular hole in the cardboard box so that the funnel fits snugly into it.

Get adult help to fix a strong light bulb to a piece of wood and hang it over the funnel as shown in the picture. A plastic cone above the bulb will protect it from sudden rain; the bulb gets very hot and cold rain drops could make it shatter. Remember that electricity is a good servant but it can be dangerous; all electrical connections must be well protected from the weather.

The moths that come to your light will hit the bulb and fall through the funnel into the box. If you put some egg-packing material in the box before setting up the light, the moths will settle down quietly and you will be able to look at them and perhaps identify some of them in the morning. Let them go when you have looked at them; scatter them amongst your garden plants so that the birds can't find them too easily.

Because cardboard is quickly damaged by moisture, it is a good idea to stand your trap on a sheet of polythene. You can also drape polythene over most of the box if you think it might rain.

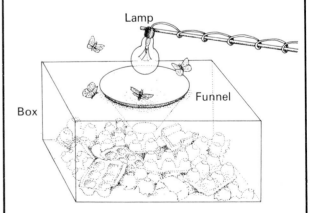

Above: A simple moth trap made from a cardboard box and a large funnel. Lots of moths will come to the trap on a warm night. Let them go when you have looked at them in the morning.

Index

Index

Index

Index

Index

Photograph Acknowledgements

HEATHER ANGEL: 20, 44 *(centre)*, 46 *(top)*, 91, 120, 126, 150
JILL CHINERY: 7 *(top)*
PAT MORRIS: 71, 96, 139 *(bottom right)*
NATURE PHOTOGRAPHERS: 14 *(bottom right)*, 42, 43, 44 *(bottom)*, 45 *(bottom)*, 63 *(top)*, 72 *(bottom)*, 73 *(top and bottom)*, 85, 93, 110, 117, 118 *(top and bottom)*, 119
NHPA: 44 *(top)*, 45 *(top)*, 62, 65, 69, 139 *(centre)*, 141
SOLARFILMA, REYKJAVIK, ICELAND: 9 *(right)*
ZEFA: 79

All other photographs: MICHAEL CHINERY